Nina Kosterina
A Young Communist in Stalinist Russia

by

Jennifer Phillips

Nina Kosterina: A Young Communist in Stalinist Russia

Publisher's Cataloging-in-Publication Data

Names: Phillips, Jennifer, author.
Title: Nina Kosterina: a young communist in Stalinist Russia / by Jennifer Phillips.
Description: Includes bibliographical references. | Second edition. | Shoreline, WA: Jennifer Phillips, 2020. | Summary: A biography of teenager Nina Kosterina, who perished fighting Germany's WWII invasion. Her published diary opened a window into the tumultuous birth of Russian Communism.
Identifiers: LCCN: 2020912834 | 978-1-7342336-7-4 (Hardcover) | ISBN 978-1-7342336-5-0 (pbk.) | 978-1-7342336-6-7 (epub)
Subjects: LCSH Kosterina, Nina, 1921-1941. | Young women--Soviet Union. | Women guerrillas--Soviet Union. | Communism--History. | Communism--Soviet Union. | YOUNG ADULT NONFICTION / Biography & Autobiography / Historical | YOUNG ADULT NONFICTION / Biography & Autobiography / Women | YOUNG ADULT NONFICTION / History / Military & Wars | HISTORY / Europe / Russia & the Former Soviet Union
Classification: LCC DK268.K62 P55 2020| DDC 914.7/03/8420924--dc23

Copyright © 2020 by Jennifer J. Phillips.

Second Edition 978-1-7342336-5-0

Cover design by Design by Roberta Morris (Leave It to 'Berta)

Printed in USA

Contents

Translation Notes	5
Diary of an Ordinary Girl	6
A Brief Chronology	12
Schooling as a Revolutionary	17
Joining the Party	34
Cherishing Family and City Life	48
Living Under Suspicion and Terror	72
Pursuing a Passion for Art	102
Juggling Friendships and Romance	126
Transforming From Student to Soldier	154
Rebuilding After the War	181
Glossary	204
Notes on Key Sources	209
About the Author	214

Nina posing in her partisan soldier's uniform as she prepared to fight against Germany

Translation Notes

Quotes and diary entries from Nina's family were translated from Russian by different professionals. The English phrasing may seem a little off at times but I have left the translated English as is to avoid misinterpreting any meanings.

Also, you will see that Nina's father has a last name of Kosterin, while her name is Kosterina. These represent the masculine and feminine versions of the name per Russian grammar rules. Nouns ending in a consonant are typically masculine, while nouns ending in "a" are typically feminine.

Diary of an Ordinary Girl

My Will

If I should not return, give all my personal papers to Lena.

I have a single thought: perhaps my action will save father?

Lena!

To you and Grisha, my only friends, I leave all my personal belongings— my diary and letters from my friends.

Lena, dear Lena, why did you leave, I want so much to see you.

Nina

> Final entry in her diary at age 20,
> November 14, 1941

Nina Kosterina penned this simple will and other final thoughts while hidden away in her family's cramped, abandoned Moscow apartment. Bombs chipped away all around her, destroying centuries-old buildings and taking lives. She blocked out the sounds of incoming artillery and nerve-rattling air-raid sirens while fretting about her two best friends, Lena Gershman and Grisha Grinblat. She didn't know where they were. She could only hope they were safe.

The German army was less than twenty miles away. Most citizens had fled to the country and other cities, including Nina's mother, sisters and Lena.

Nina insisted on staying in Moscow to prepare as a guerrilla soldier in the Red Army. Grisha was already in the fight, making her envious that she wasn't shoulder-to-shoulder with him on the battlefield.

She felt lonely and fearful, even as she ignored passionate pleas to turn back sent by her lover, a young man left behind in a student camp outside the city.

"It seems like a paradox, but it is true: this is why I am going to the front—because living is such joy, because I want so much to live, to work, to create…to live, to live!" she wrote.

She wove in reflections about her father, who fought to help the Communists gain power under Vladimir Lenin but was now imprisoned by dictator Joseph Stalin's regime as a "dangerous social element."

"On November 16th, I am joining a partisan detachment. And so my life is entering upon the path my father traveled…"

Nina then tucked her diary into a pile of her meager belongings, hid them away in the apartment and waited to begin her dangerous mission.

Two days later at noon, she joined others near Moscow's Coliseum Movie House and left for the combat zone. Nina's time as a soldier was short. By the end of December, she had perished in what became one of the bloodiest wars of all times.

What survived was her diary, providing an inspirational window into the unedited feelings, hopes and experiences of a teen who considered herself a run-of-the mill, dark-haired, dark-eyed, plain-looking girl.

"Thinking of how untalented I am, I decided to call my diary 'The Diary of an Ordinary Girl,'" Nina wrote in her first entry.

But the diary, written moment to moment with no goal of ever being published, revealed Nina as a girl bursting with emotion, energy and courage. Even though she lived in a society where citizens had few choices, she still chose to be guided by her intelligence, idealism and commitment to honesty.

The diary also offered a unique view of the grand social experiment playing out in Russia.

Nina was born at a historic moment as the Bolsheviks launched their new government. She then lived in the thick of history as the country tumbled through Stalin's tightening dictatorship and war began to loom on the horizon. While Nina transformed from a young girl to a young woman, Russia transformed from a country full of revolutionary determination to a ravaged police state with fearful, oppressed citizens forced into war.

She relished her study of Marxism and work with the Young Communist League, but she struggled with issues of truth and patriotism as Stalin's paranoia began to tear apart her family and friends.

Could she live her ideals and be a proud Russian while also serving a government that became more confusing and dangerous each day?

An ordinary girl? Perhaps. An extraordinary life? Definitely.

A Brief Chronology

Nina's story is best told around different features of her life rather than as a straightforward chronology. But here is a brief chronological unfolding to provide a timeline perspective.

April 8, 1921—Nina is born in a revolutionary camp along the Caspian Sea, about six months after the four-year Russian Civil War ended and as the Red Army invasion of other territories was concluding

1922—Nina's family moves back to Moscow

January 1924—Founding Soviet Union leader Vladimir Lenin dies, triggering a power struggle for top leadership of the young government

December 1925—Nina's sister Lelya (also known as Elena) is born

1928—Soviet Union leader Joseph Stalin launches his sweeping Five-Year Plan to industrialize the country

February 1929—Bolshevik leader Leon Trotsky is expelled from the Soviet Union, clearing the way for unchallenged rule by Joseph Stalin

April 8, 1936—Nina starts her diary

June 1936—Nina is accepted into the Young Communist League called the Komsomol

September 1936—Nina's youngest sister Vera is born and Nina's father is sent to the Russian Far East on a work assignment

Late 1936-Early 1937—Nina begins strong but stormy friendships with Grisha and Lena

December 1937—Nina's father is expelled from the Communist Party and his job

November 1939—After a fight with the government about her "suspicious" family, Nina is allowed to enroll as a college student in the Institute of Geology

November 1940—Nina's father is sentenced to a prison gulag as a "socially dangerous element"

June 22, 1941—Germany invades Russia

Fall 1941—Nina's mother and sisters evacuate to a safe zone

October 24, 1941—Nina returns to Moscow from a student geology camp

November 14, 1941—Nina departs from Moscow for the frontline as a partisan soldier

December 1941—Nina dies during a German attack while on a secret mission

1943—Nina's mother and sisters return to Moscow

1955—Nina's father returns to Moscow

February 1956—The Soviet Union's new leader, Nikita Khrushchev, denounces Stalin in a secret speech that later becomes public as he starts allowing citizens to share their experiences from the Stalin years

December 1962—Nina's diary is published in the Russian magazine, Novy Mir

1964—Nina's diary is released as a Russian book

June 1968—The English book version of Nina's diary is released, with additional printings released through 1977

November 10, 1968—Nina's father dies

1974—Nina's mother dies

Schooling as a Revolutionary

Born in a very trying year, Nina lived through all the difficulties of the first years of the making of our state…Nina's first little bed was set up in a washtub, and then on chairs put together. And until the end of her life, until her departure for the front, the girl's bed was on an iron soldier's bunk. Nina's first shoes were sewed for her by her mother out of her father's partisan's jacket; her first garments were stitched together from her mother's old skirts and blouses.

Nina's father, Alexei Kosterin,1964
afterword in Russian version of Nina's diary

Nina was born on April 8, 1921—her mother's birthday. Her life would always be influenced by the stories and passion for revolution.

Anna Mickhailovna bathed young Nina in the chilly Caspian Sea while warships loomed in the distance. The lullabies Anna sang mixed with the rustling waves and bustling sounds of their partisan unit stationed in Baku along the coast in the Caucasus Mountains.

Four years of fighting, known as the Great Russian Civil War, had just ended. The royal monarchy was gone and the Communists were in power. The country was in a terrible state. Supplies, food and jobs were very limited.

Her father, Alexei Evgrafovich Kosterin, was a Bolshevik agitator arrested twice who spent three years in prison for his role in the uprising against the czar in 1917. He then served as a Red Army partisan soldier during the civil war and edited Communist newspapers. He met his wife through a friendship with her father, a fellow Bolshevik shot and killed by the opposing White Army. Alexei stayed connected to the family. He and Anna married during the war, sometime between 1918 and 1920. Formal marriages were rare given the circumstances, and the Kosterin family does not have a record of the official date.

Alexei Kosterin in his late 30s

Anna Kosterina as a young woman

Nina arrived when victory was fresh and a better future seemed the only possibility for Russia. And she beat the odds. Many infants died under the harsh, lean conditions of the 1920s.

Alexei moved the family in 1922 as Russia organized into the Union of Soviet Socialist Republics (USSR). "After demobilization, we had only our overcoats, one and a half changes of linen and the desire to work and learn," he wrote.

Little is known about the opinions of Nina's family during the tough economic years that followed. Her father's writings, of course, would have been carefully edited and what he later wrote about Nina's upbringing included no judgments or mention of the state policies that influenced their lives.

A Country on the Move

Russia's new leaders, the Bolsheviks, mobilized to create a society based on Marxist principles.

The Bolsheviks were the extreme left wing of the Russian Social Democratic Labour Party. Led by Vladimir Lenin through the 1917 revolution, they intended to produce a free and just society with adequate food, shelter, clothing, equality and dignity.

Women would have new freedoms. The worker and peasant population would have a strong voice. Religion would not dominate people's thinking. The Bolsheviks attacked Russia's churches and pushed for an atheist society. Russia, Lenin promised, would have a new type of dictatorship: a dictatorship of the proletariat, which meant rule by the workers, not a royal monarchy.

The Communists faced a daunting task, given the staggering size and complexity of Russia in population, geography and politics.

Russian cities in the first part of the 1920s revealed interesting contrasts.

Peasant stalls, private shops and pockets of luxury mingled with swarms of homeless children orphaned by the war and decaying city structures covered with posters and revolutionary symbols.

Peasants farming the land made up about seventy-six percent of the country's 147 million people.

Citizens of this era tried to live ordinary lives under extraordinary circumstances.

The Bolsheviks had started converting farms, factories and businesses from private to state ownership in 1917. They believed the state needed to control everything for the benefit of the people. Yet, Lenin worried as the civil war ended in 1921. Millions of people lacked work and suffered from drought and famine.

He created a New Economic Policy (NEP) that allowed people to once again own and run small farms, hire labor and own businesses or factories. This policy compromised Marxist beliefs and angered many in his new government.

Lenin admitted it was a struggle to have "state capitalism under Communism," but he defended his actions.

"During the past year, we showed quite clearly that we cannot run the economy," Lenin told the 11th

Party Congress. "That is the fundamental lesson. Either we prove the opposite in the coming year, or Soviet power will not be able to exist."

People also looked for leadership from Leon Trotsky, a deeply knowledgeable student of Marxism. Considered the key thinker behind the Bolshevik revolution, Trotsky worked to put Marxist beliefs into place through the new government.

Lenin and Trotsky were two of the primary leaders in the new Soviet Union. Joseph Stalin was the third. Together the three men launched a series of economic and political changes that touched all corners of the huge country for generations.

Soon, though, Lenin's health eroded when he suffered a series of strokes. His political power also eroded and his relationship with Stalin soured. When he died in 1924, a new collective leadership formed with Stalin, Trotsky and other men who hoped to be the Communist Party's new leader.

Stalin emerged as the winner.

Nina the Aktiv

While the country sorted out its government, Alexei worked as a journalist based out of Moscow and Nina the toddler said hello to a baby sister, Lelya, in December 1925. (Lelya also became known as Elena, which is how she is referenced in this book.)

Nina as a toddler in 1923

The family's cramped apartment became the hub for many activities shaping Nina's world. The family hosted frequent visits by Red Guard and Civil War partisan soldiers. They often stayed a month or more. Nina loved listening to their friendly, rough ways as they sang, reminisced and argued about Russian life and the revolution.

The Bolsheviks had high expectations for children.

Nina—and the millions of other children born in the 1920s—had a job to do. Their job title: aktiv, or activist. Their job duties: Help build a society of citizens who embraced
Communism, didn't believe in religion, challenged bureaucracy and corruption, knew how to read and write, and focused on community instead of individual needs.

Nina started her activist "work" in kindergarten and continued throughout her life.

Her school sat on the corner of Voravskogo and Molchanovka Streets in the heart of Moscow.

> *Unfortunately, I wasn't able to adequately observe the influence of school...on Nina, because very often I had to leave Moscow. However, even my infrequent visits to the school and conversations I had with teachers left me with good impressions...In Nina's childhood and adolescence she had no exceptional aptitude or inclination. She took to book learning in the first years with difficulty. I well remember this stage of her education.*
>
> Alexei Kosterin, 1964 afterword
> in Russian version of Nina's diary

Education as a Tool for Social Change

The Bolsheviks had to deal with three dilemmas when they took over the country:

★ How would they provide care and food for children while their parents worked in the fields and factories, especially in support of the Marxist goal to liberate women from the home?

★ How could they boost the country's literacy rate since about half of the population, mainly in rural areas, was considered illiterate in 1926?

★ How would they create a generation of new Communists?

Schools played a significant role in people's lives. Education became a main route to advancement in the new Soviet society.

The Bolsheviks required school attendance and opened all-day kindergartens to care for young children while their parents worked. Schools covered basic academics and life skills such as good nutrition, hygiene and manners while also working to make the children into "small comrades."

Despite many challenges, the Communists did eventually achieve some aspects of their goal of educating and socializing the population. For example, the country's literacy rate and the number of children in school had doubled by the late 1930s.

Nina's Schooling

Teachers told her parents she was "a clever, diligent girl, but has difficulty grasping the lessons." Nina's schoolwork struggles apparently continued until an intervention by her father. Alexei asked the school to hold Nina back from the sixth grade because her marks were only satisfactory. He said Nina agreed with his idea, even though some of the school officials considered it harsh.

"My 'partisan' experiment worked: in all of the following years Nina's learning was 'good' or 'excellent,'" Alexei wrote.

Nina persisted in her studies for the next several years, greatly inspired by revolutionary teachings, her job as an activist and her love of learning despite her early struggles. She graduated from secondary school in 1939, eager to become a geologist. But her dreams of a college education were initially dashed. Government officials denied her entrance to college when her father was arrested as a suspected anti-Stalin agitator.

"What an outrageous excuse they gave me: 'In view of lack of dormitory space…'" she angrily wrote about her situation. "They said that to me, a Moscow resident who needs no dormitory space!"

The state sent her on a depressing journey to enroll in an industrial institute in her birthplace of Baku. She reached the capital city of Azerbaijan along the western shore of the Caspian Sea only to have officials deny her admission and send her back to Moscow.

"When I returned from Baku, all hope of continuing school gone, I started thinking seriously about work," Nina wrote. "However, mother most decisively refused to hear of it: 'You have a right to an education and you must have it. You will go to school!' And yet once more I saw the flinty strength of mama's character."

Anna wrote a stern letter of complaint to Stalin himself.

"On what basis," she asked in the letter, "are they violating the principle that you have proclaimed yourself: 'The son is not responsible for his father?'"

Whether Stalin actually read the letter is unknown, but the Committee of Higher Education called in Anna and she returned with Nina's note for admission to the Institute of Geology.

"I will be a geologist—my dream is coming true!" Nina penned in describing the turn of events. She enrolled in the fall of 1939 and studied until the war halted schoolwork in the fall of 1941.

Nina was not alone in being energized by the revolutionary vision to build a socialist society.

One man who was a "small comrade" reflected on his experience later in life: "In spite of material difficulties, such as the constant food shortage which was particularly acute at the time, neither I nor the young people around me, had any anti-Soviet feelings. We simply found in the heroic tension involved in the building of a new world an excuse for all the difficulties…"

Nina fit this description. She took pride in her schoolwork and pride in her activism.

She was on a path to emerge as a young Bolshevik leader herself who could pass along the teachings to a new generation of Soviets.

Joining the Party

There was a lot of anxiety in connection with my admission to the Komsomol. I have, generally, been reading the newspapers, but all the same I had to go to father for help. He talked to me for two hours, reminding me about many things and explaining others, especially about the Constitution. After the talk with him, I went to the District Committee of the Komsomol quite calmly. What a father I have! There were ten of us at the District Committee, and everybody was nervous.

I did not like the District Committee office: dirty, with smudged, dingy walls, nowhere to sit down. It seemed to me that I was calm, but others said that I came out of the office white as chalk. They gave me a membership card, tiny, tiny, white.

At home, I showed it to papa. He caught me in his arms and threw me up and kissed me. 'Good girl,

Ninok!' He said it in such a way that I was filled with joy and pride.

> Nina's Diary, June 20, 1936

The Communists wanted more young members. With her father's good standing as a Bolshevik revolutionary, Nina apparently faced no difficulties in being accepted. First she joined the Little Octoberists for children ages eight to eleven. Then she joined the Young Pioneers, the branch for ages nine to fourteen. The Komsomol was the Communist Youth party for ages fourteen to twenty-eight.

Uniforms and a military-style structure were used to instill pride and purpose in young members. The Pioneers, for example, wore a red kerchief with white tops and black trousers. The kerchief's three points represented the indestructible friendship of three generations—the Communists, young Communists and Pioneers. Ten Pioneers members formed a link. Two to four links formed a detachment. Several detachments formed a brigade, which included links of Little Octoberists. Komsomol members had a quasi-military uniform, described in one history book as "knickers, botinki (boots), stockings, semi-military tunic, belt and a sam-brown belt (worn diagonally across the chest from shoulder to hip)."

Even with her solid Bolshevik background, securing a place in the Komsomol was a big deal for Nina. Gaining and keeping membership in the party youth branches proved difficult. Suspicion about a child's family or heritage prevented membership. Stories of rejection were common, such as one about a teenage girl denied a membership because her grandmother spoke fluent French, suggesting a bourgeoisie connection. The unit leader argued that "all knowledge can be used in the service of the revolution" but the girl was rejected anyway.

Tough Times Under a Dictatorship

Happy moments were extremely precious. Life had already been tough throughout the country. Under Stalin, it got worse. Within a few years after Lenin's death, Stalin had exiled Trotsky and developed what historians call a "cult of personality." The country's tallest mountain carried Stalin's name, along with many cities, towns and villages. The Soviet national anthem even included his name. Stalin's pictures and posters peppered the land.

Lenin's policies had made more food available and helped the economy, but they also produced a new class of small family farm owners who became known as kulaks, which translates into "tightwad." Perceptions grew that the kulaks were wealthy and greedy.

Stalin announced his First Five-Year Plan in 1928 and launched the "Great Change" felt by the entire population. The state immediately seized farms to become collective homes and working places for peasants.

Profits from farming paid for electric power stations, mines, dams, canals and factories. The state assigned workers their jobs and living space. Officials distributed food to those who could show they worked in a government-approved factory or business. They sent many citizens to work on collective farms in remote parts of the country.

A wave of terror began. Millions of kulaks resisted having their farms collectivized. They were shot, hanged or sent to labor camps. Millions more died when the government took their grain and created a famine. Stalin's regime encouraged peasants to inform on their neighbors if they looked better off and weren't following the new policies. "Dekulakization" became the word used to describe liquidation of the kulaks.

Meanwhile, the Communist vision included an abundance of food for everyone, but it materialized only for certain officials and privileged citizens.

Trotsky, from his place in exile, accused Stalin of betraying the revolution by allowing a privileged class. Others certainly agreed, but they could not openly share their anger as Trotsky did.

Daily living became a survival skill. Consumer goods were hard to find and poor quality. Until 1935, the government outlawed artisan crafts such as baking, sausage-making, tailoring, dress-making, laundering, hairdressing, shoe repair, and plumbing. A common sight involved thousands of people waiting in lines for basics such as bread, clothing and shoes. The importance of "blat" or friendship networks created a second economy that helped citizens survive the harsh conditions.

A Stalin quote served as a state slogan splashed around the country on posters and other materials: "Life has become better, comrades; life has become more cheerful." Citizens angrily found irony in the quote, although they were certain to express their true thoughts carefully.

In the late 1930s, Stalin eased up a bit. He allowed farmers to keep their own houses and tools. They also could grow food in private gardens for their own use. The government stopped rationing bread, promised to produce more consumer goods and started encouraging leisure activities along with a more cultured atmosphere.

Citizens took the changes with relief but also wariness. Suddenly, it was okay for them to own material goods. What if Stalin changed his mind and then punished them?

Stalin also introduced a second Five-Year Plan aimed at producing military arms. The threat of war began dominating the Russian landscape, giving citizens one more item on their long list of worries and struggles.

Life in the Komsomol

Times grew even harsher and more dangerous in the country.

Nina did periodically write about the political situation, but she never mentioned challenges such as finding food, tight living quarters and other basics. Millions of citizens didn't survive this era, including Nina's paternal grandfather, a long-time Bolshevik loyalist who starved to death during the winter of 1931-1932.

Evgraf Kosterin, Nina's grandfather

Nina often described school and friendships in relationship to her young Communist activities. She tapped her conscience frequently to sort through right and wrong while navigating the blend of old and new rules emerging in the Soviet society.

Everything she wrote and did seemed shaped by the Bolshevik vision and her role.

Once, Nina wrote to a friend proudly explaining how she was one of only seven Komsomol members in her school, juggling a heavy workload but also enjoying "a lot of prestige."

Youth Communist members were groomed to feel like heroes with a duty to challenge bureaucrats, corruption and religion. "Unmasking" suspected spies of the state became a sport to many, although Nina never shared any stories about doing this and her writings suggest she found this task revolting.

Outside the city, the young Communists were expected to help collectivize property. This, plus their focus on eliminating religion, often put them at odds with rural residents, who called the Pioneers' tie the "devil's noose" and sometimes attacked youth brigades.

Despite the military structure, officials dealt with much wild behavior among the Communist Party youth, especially in rural regions. These kids considered joining the party a possible ticket out of isolation and poverty, yet they often were less loyal to the cause.

Nina had no patience for unruly Komsomol behavior and incompetent leaders.

"We were alone among the unorganized, undisciplined mass of kids," she wrote in describing how she arrived to lead a camp of younger members in

September 1938. "The director was an incompetent weakling, and his assistant Valya did not contribute much either."

Otherwise, Nina enjoyed her Komsomol duties. She participated in Marxist reading discussions, taught Young Pioneers, created educational displays and materials, and trained through military marches.

She had a special fondness for teaching Young Pioneers. She loved children and enjoyed getting affectionate letters from her young students.

"I've gotten to love many of the children and will remember them for a long time, perhaps always," she wrote after leading a summer camp unit of twenty-five children.

The Communist way also emphasized the need to critically assess one's own weaknesses while boldly calling out character strengths and weaknesses in others. Nina readily adopted this philosophy.

> *Yesterday we had a Komsomol meeting. It lasted from eight in the evening until two in the morning. The subject on the agenda was 'Criticism and Self-criticism.' The director gave us a short report on Stalin's speech on this question. Then we began to offer criticism. The director got most of it. And for good reason. A stick-in-the-mud, not a director. I also spoke and attacked him. I said everything that had been on my mind for a long time—about the poor discipline, about our section leader, and about him personally. It was a good speech. I got my share of criticism too: they said that I've stopped paying attention to my schoolwork, and so on. They are right. I really haven't been doing anything lately . . .*

Nina's Diary, April 17, 1937

Nina identified strongly with her Komsomol membership. And when the going got tough, she would often wander the streets of Moscow deep in thought, using the Marxist techniques of self-reflection and self-criticism to stay true to her ideals.

Cherishing Family and City Life

There was a lively song that was always ringing out in our family. A simple Russian song. And not on a gramophone record–we sang ourselves. I have loved Russian songs since I was a child. When Nina was a toddler, it was a great pleasure for me, putting her to bed, to walk around the apartment with her and sing…When it seemed that my daughter was falling asleep, I lowered my voice to a whisper. Still half asleep, she would often demand: 'Sing, Alyosha, sing.'

Alexei Kosterin, 1964 afterword
in Russian version of Nina's diary

"Thank You, Comrade Stalin, For Our Happy Childhood" became a familiar message on posters in schools around the country. Whether Nina and her family agreed with this slogan, she did benefit from the government's approach. She had a home and enough to eat, a steady education and the chance to advance her social position through membership in the Communist Party's youth branches.

Living in the heart of Russia with a protective family and city conveniences not available in many parts of the country gave Nina strength. However, even these fundamental features of life would prove fragile.

Nina held a constant thread of affection for her father. The relationship with her mother seemed to include more conflict, with Nina wavering between affection and contempt as her mother took primary responsibility for the family when Alexei was detained by Stalin's secret police. Elena and Nina seemed close and, by 1936, they had a younger sister, Vera.

Nina's grandmothers served as the family matriarchs. Her maternal grandmother lived with them in Moscow. Nina's diary entries paint the picture of a woman frequently in tears and worn down by the stress of their situation. Nina affectionately called her paternal grandmother Petrovaskaya Babushka (grandmother) in honor of her home city, Petrovsky. Her visits included entertaining Nina with a love of books, Ukrainian songs and stories about her activities during the civil war.

Meanwhile, Moscow functioned like an extended member of the family for Nina—a centuries-old, swarming hub of humanity that became a key character in her life. She had a front seat in the grand renovation of Moscow. She did not take it for granted as she grew up.

Reconstruction of the Capital

For two hundred years, St. Petersburg served as Russia's capital city. Then the new Soviet rulers moved the capital back to Moscow after the Bolshevik revolution.

The Soviets intended to make Moscow a prototype for a new model city to be copied in other parts of the country and world. Russians flocked to Moscow from the countryside and other cities. In 1920, the city had 1 million residents. By 1933, the population was 3.4 million and by 1960, it was 6 million.

The rapid and unrelenting growth created the sense that Moscow was the country's main hub, but it also created a never-ending strain on the city's infrastructure.

Even so, Moscow did become a showcase city compared to the rest of the Soviet Union. Plans, blueprints and models for the "General Plan for the Reconstruction of Moscow" were posted throughout the city.

Citizens jammed sidewalks, packed streetcars and lived with unpredictable electricity, but they at least had access to basics not available in many other parts of Russia. They had buses, trams and trolleys to get around town, and even running water and sewage systems.

One showpiece in the quest to modernize—the Moscow Metro—began opening rail lines in the early 1930s, with escalators leading riders to and from beautiful underground stations with murals and chandeliers.

A famous French architect, Le Corbusier, wrote about what he witnessed while traveling to Russia: "This country builds, and needs to build. Everywhere, from one end of the country to the other, but principally in Moscow and Leningrad, a whole nation stands in need of amenities."

City officials shifted and converted buildings on the famous Gorky Street to give it a new look. They turned palaces into cultural centers. Officials hired an American to remake Gorky Park into a prototype "park of culture and rest" for the country. The redesigned park featured many recreational activities, such as dance floors, cinemas, bowling alleys, Ferris wheels, a parachute jump and agitational corners.

Churches also became a target for remodeling due to the rejection of religion by the government. Officials closed, demolished or claimed many buildings for non-religious uses while scrapping thousands of religious objects such as bells, candelabras and artwork. Much centuries-old history was lost in this conversion to a modern Communist state.

Stalin involved himself in the details of Moscow's development. His loyalists even tried—unsuccessfully—to have the city's name changed, with ideas including Great Stalin City, Stalin City-Moscow, Stalin's Bounty and Stalin.

Living in the Hub

Nina's family lived on Trubnikovsky Lane, about a mile from the stone wall entryway to the Kremlin and Red Square, in a building later occupied by a government office. They were ringed by three churches and had quick access to the bustling Smolensky Market where Alexei and Anna shopped and bought Nina many books.

This location placed them at the heart of the city, with buildings and streets then moving outward in ever-widening protective circles to form the rest of Moscow city proper.

Nina's sister Elena recalled that the big house where they lived was broken into apartments. The Kosterins' space was sure to be tiny. Elena remembered it was unusual and interesting, with high ceilings, oak trim, an

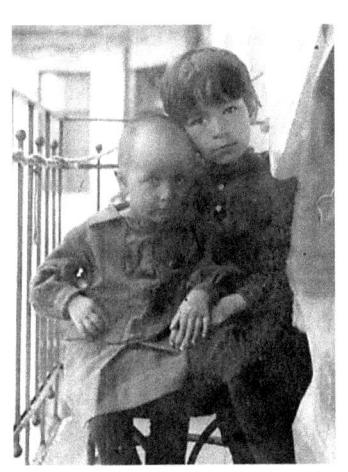

Little sister Elena at age 3 with Nina at age 7 at their Moscow home

old wine cellar and a small courtyard inside its walls.

"It was constructed by the architect Malinovski in 1912," Elena said in a 2004 interview. "In the 1920s Stalin organized the People's Committee for Nations here. Employees of this committee were settled there with their families. These were people of different nationalities…We lived in the communal apartment. This apartment had a kitchen and toilet facilities shared by a number of tenants. Jews, Germans, Russians and a Tartar resided here all together…We lived very friendly in our apartment, always helped each other."

Handicrafts filled the tiny Kosterin apartment from Alexei's work travels—items made of stone, shell, coral, wood and birch bark, along with hand-painted spoons, bowls, flagons and a little table with two stools. "As a journalist, I often had to leave Moscow. For Nina, letters and gifts from the road were like a living, subjective geography," Alexei wrote.

The apartment served as a base for frequent visitors.

Uncle Vasia liked to visit and tell Nina battle stories from the revolution. Uncle Seryozha helped Nina with math problems. Cousins Stella and Irma often came to play. And another family friend called "Khudoga" influenced Nina's love of the arts, her father wrote. Khudoga taught Nina art history during his visits, took her to exhibitions and left behind his own sketches, cartoons and pictures as gifts.

Finding a Spot to Call Home

For most Moscow residents, finding any spot to call home was a significant challenge. Urban planners neglected residential housing construction. Buildings also became state property after the revolution, with housing officials deciding how much space residents got.

Many families, like Nina's, lived in communal apartments with one family to a room. Others lived in dormitories and barracks. Even more people, including whole families, lived in hallways, corners of kitchens and public spaces.

There was little sense of privacy. Bathrooms were rare and strangers, often from very different backgrounds, suddenly became roommates. The communal living situation forced by Bolshevik politics and the housing shortage usually produced more stress among citizens than it did warm feelings of a collective society.

One Moscow resident described the typical communal apartment like this: "The room had no running water; sheets or curtains marked off sub areas where two or three generations slept and sat; food dangled out of winter windows in sacks. Shared sinks, toilets, washtubs, and cooking facilities (usually nothing more than Primus wood alcohol burners and cold water taps) lay either in a no-man's land between the dwelling rooms or down an unheated, laundry-festooned hallway. A hot scrubbing was had at a public bath once a week in winter, twice in summer. Muscovites who lived this way felt fortunate, for a great many did worse."

Living conditions were grim, and yet they were better in Moscow than most parts of the country.

A Strange and Dangerous Childhood

Moscow bubbled over with colorful people and colorful living. As a pre-teenager, Nina had big eyes and big ears—she drank in the variety of grown-up behaviors around her without a strong sense of good versus bad.

Her family grew worried when she picked up some of the rougher habits she saw in the "tradesmen and hoodlums" around the city, wrote her father. "Fortunately, we detected this pretty quickly and, with the aid of the tenants of our crowded communal apartment and neighbors in our housing complex, we broke the influence of the street."

Nina may or may not have appreciated the concern of her family and larger community of neighbors. It took this type of interest, though, to help children survive the 1930s. Through many different combinations of circumstances, not every child was so lucky.

Growing up in the 1930s as a Soviet youth included a dizzying assortment of activities and issues.

Soviet children had their heroes. Aviators, polar explorers and border guards were among the most popular. They also participated in activities ranging from normal to ominous.

Student life could include any combination of studying, political work, dancing, drinking, sex, spying on neighbors or forcing citizens to give up private property.

City and village streets rang with the laughter of youth groups innocently enjoying folk tunes and accordion music or rebelliously trying out modern "western" music and the fox trot. Gangs fought, shouted and harassed people. Rhythmic military beats punctuated the air as young Communists marched in lockstep during parade and training routines.

Soviet youth enjoyed new chances to learn and build their skills, but the state decided what they did. Opportunities came with little freedom of choice.

Children faced enormous stresses merely trying to move through everyday life. Severe food, housing and clothing shortages took a toll. But perhaps even worse, many children were pressured to publicly denounce their parents when the grownups were arrested. They paid for the "sins" of their parents in terms of opportunities and even freedom or their lives. Joseph Stalin finally declared this shouldn't be the case. Even then, some people followed Stalin's new philosophy and some did not.

Similar to political beliefs changing without notice, social customs and programs flip-flopped through the years. A chief debate involved the role of family and marriage in a socialist society. Were these useless leftovers from the old world or important strategies to create a stable Russian life?

A Strong Sense of Family

Nina enjoyed frequent outings with her sister Elena and cousins Stella and Irma.

"Nina was very strong physically," Elena recalled. "She had a sturdy, wide turn of her shoulders. She swam very good, played volleyball, was very fond of sports." Elena and Stella stayed in touch as adults and liked to reminisce about their childhood. They remember an outing to Gorky Park in Moscow when Nina parachuted off a tower while they waited trembling at the top, knowing Nina expected them to go next.

On a country outing in 1929 or 1930: Elena, age 4, Nina, age 9 and Stella at age 5

Nina encouraged them to try different sports.

"She tried to teach us to swim. Unfortunately, neither Stella nor me could do it. I almost drowned twice but did not learn to swim. Nina was opposite, as if born in the water…"

Moscow had much to offer a teenager like Nina. "For Nina,

newspapers, magazines, books, the theatre, trips to museums, to exhibitions, to the woods outside Moscow, to the Volga—all were a big school," wrote Alexei.

Red Square, which actually is rectangular and has no red stones, hosted massive military and citizen parades. Special days included May 1 to celebrate International Labor Day and November 7 to celebrate the Bolshevik revolution.

Nina liked being swept up in the excitement and chaos of these events.

> *. . . I jumped up early, feeling marvelous. We had tea with grandmother's cakes. Then off to school. Stayed there until eleven, and then went to the Institute of Law. The students were no longer there, but we managed to find them later in a kind of dead-end block off Hertzen Street. We sang and danced for an hour and a half to the music of an accordion. At two, we*

> *went to Red Square. I saw Stalin. There was some confusion beyond the square. We were caught in a crush in a narrow street and were swept along…We looked at the stands of the food industries, then we wanted to dance, but there was too much of a crush. We went on to Theatre Square. I liked Stalin's portrait, about as big as the Mostorg Building. On the way back we stopped off at the Manege Square and danced our fill. I came home at eleven, with aching feet.*
>
> Nina's Diary, November 7, 1936

Nina and her family also enjoyed the rivers that flow through and around Moscow.

The Volga River, the longest in Europe, runs north and east of the city. "Mother Volga" has been called the cultural heart of Russia.

Some city families had country dachas, or vacation homes, that they visited on holidays. This was a sign of privilege, due to wealth or their job in the new government. Elena said her family did not have access to a dacha but instead stayed with a writer friend of their father's at his country home.

"Almost every summer we went to the city of Khvolynsk, a small city on the Volga River," Elena recalled. "The water was cold, just icy. We fell down to a spring and drank this water. Khvolynsk was buried in gardens. These were famous Khvolynsk gardens."

The family's summer holiday trips outside Moscow started even as Nina was very young, creating a lifetime passion for the outdoors. She would grow up always relishing time spent in the woods, camping and boating on the Volga River.

> *A trip to the Volga, when she had reached eight years of age, made a tremendous impression on Nina. The Volga, the Khvalynsk*

Mountains, the forests and gardens, the secret little chapels in the gorges near springs...These trips, repeated for several years, developed and reinforced in her a love for Russian nature, for Russian songs, the Russian language and our whole way of life.

Alexei Kosterin, 1964 afterword
in Russian version of Nina's diary

Nina (far right) and her mother (middle) on a trip to the Volga in 1936

Nina reflected on the "pleasant melancholy" she felt about the Volga as she captured the words of a revolutionary song regarding the river:

Many songs have been sung of the Volga,
But the tunes of those songs were not gay,
In the old days our sorrow was singing,
It's our joy that is singing today.
Our own, beloved, beautiful
As bounteous as the sea,
Free as our own homeland,
Wide, deep and strong and free…

The Moskva River, which winds like a snake through the city curving in to brush the city center, also served as a constant in Nina's life. She swam in its chilly waters and enjoyed romantic strolls along its banks with her first love, Grisha. And she frequented Moscow's many museums, libraries, parks and theaters. She took these outings seriously, documenting her visits and assessments of places such as the Museum of Fine Arts, Kamerny Theatre, Tretyakov Art Gallery, the Writer's House, Hall of Columns,

Maly Theatre, Lenin Library, Bolshoi Theatre, Red Army Theatre, Gorky Park, Stanislavsky's Theatre and Tretyakov Gallery.

A Crumbling World

Even Nina's strong home life couldn't withstand the terror to come, first from her own government and then from the violent forces of war fueled by a German dictator with a desire to take over the vast Russian lands. Her poetic descriptions of Moscow became a lasting tribute to her love for the city that was home for her short life.

> *I love Moscow. Last night I had insomnia. I turned from side to side for a long time, trying to fall asleep. Then I got up quietly, dressed, and went out. It was after three. Silent, deserted streets, a fine, bracing frost...I walked without aim and without choosing direction. Crossed*

the center of town. The Red Square, the Kremlin and scarlet flag over it—I saw it all with new eyes and with a new feeling. I cannot even define what I felt at the time. There are no words. What a pity I don't know music. Only a solemn symphony could probably express the emotions, moods, and vague images that took possession of me at that silent hour before dawn...Moscow! The very word stirs me and fills my soul with pride, with the rhythms of ancient songs and epic tales.

                              Nina's Diary, January 20, 1940

Living Under Suspicion and Terror

... I was elected to the Komsomol committee. Recently we took up the case of one of the girls. Her mother and father had been arrested. At first I disagreed with the motion to expel her, but later, the others convinced me, and I voted for the expulsion. Still, I am not certain that she should have been expelled. The girl cried, she did not want to leave the Komsomol, but at the same time she said that she loved her mother and father and would never repudiate them. After the meeting, I felt terrible, and when I came home I cried for a long time. How is it her fault if her parents were arrested for something? Come back soon, papa, if you can. It is dreary and lonely at home without you...

Nina's Diary, September 13, 1937
contents of a letter to her father

On a spring day in 1938, Nina and her family received a surprise visitor. Uncle Misha appeared in their apartment, released by Stalin's secret police after being arrested with his wife more than a year earlier.

A proud Bolshevik revolutionary who had done well in the new Party structure, the oldest brother of Nina's father now sat confused and frightened. He whispered and looked over his shoulder as he told Nina, her mother and grandmother about terrible things going on around the country.

They didn't know the whereabouts of his wife, Anya. The police had sent their daughter, Irma, to an orphanage.

By this time, the Communists had also expelled her father's middle brother, Uncle Vasia, for supposedly saying he liked Lenin better than Stalin. Her mother's brother, Uncle Ilya, had disappeared while working in the mines. The family eventually figured out he was in a prison camp.

Nina had watched their landlords arrested—a scene played out repeatedly around the country as secret police arrived, gave the accused person a little time to gather belongings, and then whisked him or her away as tearful family members stood by.

And, during all of this, Nina's father waited to learn whether he would be arrested in the Russian Far East. The Party expelled him with the accusation that he was in contact with his brothers and other old revolutionaries now declared enemies of the state.

Nina's family was unraveling, caught up in what became known as the Great Purges of 1937 and 1938.

Political Dream Gone Wrong

The tide had turned from the 1920s, when the government allowed more debate and passion for revolution. Citizens expressed serious intellectual interest in Marxism and Leninism.

By the 1930s, however, paying too much attention to political theory could be dangerous. Family members, friends, neighbors or coworkers could disappear based on a vague accusation or casual comment.

Russia became a full police state where citizens had few rights. Political terror expanded.

Police started by arresting past leaders and non-believers. Then they focused on people suspected of challenging Stalin and supporting Leon Trotsky, who was exiled in 1928 after becoming a sharp critic of Stalin's leadership. Even old Bolshevik revolutionary families were no longer safe. The rules of proper behavior shifted constantly. No one knew who to trust or how to act.

The political movement unfolding in Russia over this period evolved in four phases.

First, the Bolshevik revolutionary group seized control of the government and eliminated royal rule in 1917. Vladimir Lenin returned from exile to lead the new Bolshevik government.

Then, other groups fighting for control of the country refused to accept Bolshevik authority. The Bolsheviks responded with force, creating a first version of the Communist secret police called the Cheka. They purged anyone opposing the Bolsheviks and executed Czar Nicholas II and his family, who had been under house arrest since the 1917 uprising. The Bolsheviks forced citizens to enlist in the Red Army and made peasants give up most of their food to feed the new army. They executed those who refused.

The four-year civil war of 1918-1921 followed as the Red Army and opposing White Army fought for control of the country.

In the third phase of transformation, the Bolsheviks won and Lenin established the USSR and Communist government, with Trotsky and Stalin as his two top leaders.

Each stage of Russia's evolution contained fear and brutality packaged as visions for a bright future. Life under Stalin, however, created the most dramatic and disturbing picture of the Russian Communist dream gone wrong. And it is the period that turned Nina's family from proud revolutionaries into accused enemies of the government they helped to establish.

Nina's grandparents, uncles and father all were actively involved in the Bolshevik movement.

Alexei became interested in revolutionary ideas while working in a cement factory as a young man in the city of Volsk. He was arrested for distributing banned literature and organizing agitators. After his release, he moved to Moscow, assumed a different name and began collaborating again with the Bolsheviks. He faced a second arrest. After his release, the Bolsheviks sent him to Baku to continue organizing new members. The White Army arrested Alexei in 1919, but he escaped from prison and served in the Red Army for the rest of the civil war.

Alexei's Path to State Enemy

Nina's father and uncles fell into the category of old Bolsheviks that Stalin wanted to get rid of so they wouldn't challenge his regime.

Nina monitored the political events and, in January 1937, wrote in her diary about a Trotskyite trial under way. She theorized that the defendants all would be shot. "How could it happen that old revolutionaries who had fought for decades for a people's government became enemies of the people?"

Even though her father was a loyal revolutionary soldier and journalist who continued to work as a party activist, the tone of one Moscow directory referencing his writing in 1931 suggested he was falling out of good favor with authorities. He seemed caught in whatever new politics were unfolding. An unspoken fear about his situation hung over the family.

Nina confessed her soul searching in her diary.

"Something strange is happening. I thought and thought, and came to the conclusion: if my father also turns out to be a Trotskyite and an enemy of his country, I shall not be sorry for him! I wrote this, but (I confess) there is a gnawing worm of doubt…"

Stalin's Passion for Purges

Controls that Lenin started became tighter and more brutal under Stalin. The Red Terror began. At first, profession and family background determined a person's fate.

To be labeled a bourgeois meant you were politically unreliable and holding on to the wrong beliefs. Priests and people with past wealth or upper-class ties were at most risk, along with people holding white-collar or intellectual jobs.

"We are exterminating the bourgeoisie as a class," instructed one district chairman of the secret police agency. "During the investigation, do not look for evidence that the accused acted in deed or word against Soviet power. The first questions that you ought to put are: To what class does he belong? What is his origin? What is his education or profession? And it is these questions that ought to determine the fate of the accused. In this lies the significance and essence of the Red Terror."

Stalin also wanted to get rid of old or new Bolsheviks whose reputations could make them challengers. In 1927, Trotsky and 1,500 other "Trotskyites" were expelled from the party.

A year later, the secret police arrested and exiled Trotsky. He moved through Central Asia, Turkey, France, Norway and Mexico over the next twelve years, continuing to challenge Stalin from afar. Stalin believed Trotsky was organizing a conspiracy to overthrow him and return the country to capitalism.

"We have internal enemies. We have external enemies. This, comrades, must not be forgotten for a single moment," Stalin warned the country.

Negative feelings began surfacing against Stalin, but disagreement was seen as treason and terrorism. A culture emerged where people thought one thing and carefully said another.

Stalin used the assassination of a popular Communist official in 1934 to claim there was a serious plot under way.

He warned citizens in a speech that the USSR was "encircled by hostile powers whose agents, recruited from Troskyites with party cards and hiding behind Bolshevik masks, had penetrated all party, governmental, and economic organizations and were engaged in wrecking and espionage, not stopping short of murder."

Stalin ordered mass arrests to squash the feared coup. Many people faced prompt death sentences as the great purges got under way. At least half a million party members were expelled, even if their only "crime" was not denouncing others who had been accused. Friends and neighbors avoided expelled members. The secret police and state officials encouraged wives to divorce accused husbands, or they arrested wives of the most important enemies.

Children of arrested parents went to orphanages under different names unless relatives came forward immediately to take legal guardianship, but to do this was risky to those relatives. Children of arrested parents also could be expelled from university or high school, usually after being publicly humiliated and pressured to denounce their parents.

The purging also included top commanders in the Red Army and thousands of officers—an act that haunted Stalin later during World War II when the Germans attacked.

Historians believe hundreds of thousands were shot during the purges under Stalin.

Most trials of ordinary citizens occurred in secret. Confessions usually were forced through torture or the "conveyor" method in which a series of interrogators would work to wear down a person over hours or days. Police also used threats against the accused person's family to break him or her down. Punishment could extend down to children of age twelve for crimes committed by parents.

A Turn for the Worse

Alexei had left on a work assignment for the Russian Far East in September 1936. "For two years now, we shall be without the companion of our frequent surprise outings in the country, which father was so clever at thinking up," Nina wrote as she described mobs of friends and colleagues coming to the apartment to wish him farewell.

But as trouble started to brew, Alexei sent home a telegram in September 1937 saying he might return early.

From left: Elena, Anna, Vera and Nina in 1937

Meanwhile, telegrams from Aunt Marina to Uncle Ilya were coming back "Undelivered." The women took all of this as a bad sign and Nina vowed to stand by her father.

In December 1937, Nina received a letter back from her father sharing that the Party had expelled him and dismissed him from his job. "I shall not go into details: at your age much will still be unclear to you," he wrote. "But you must remember one thing: you will need a great deal of calm and endurance now. I do not know as yet how events will turn for me. But even in the worst case, you must be sure that your father was never a scoundrel or double-dealer, and has never blemished his name by anything dirty or base…"

Nina wrote in her diary: "He is accused of contacts with his brothers and with many of those who have now been declared enemies of the people—Bukharin, Radek, and others. Before the Revolution, papa knew many people in the revolutionary movement, and now he is blamed for it. What am I, a total fool, not to understand this?"

Alexei associated with pivotal figures in the country's revolutionary history.

Nikolai Bukharin was a high-level Communist official and editor of Pravda, the official Communist party newspaper. Stalin arrested him in 1937 after Bukharin protested Stalin's actions to give himself unlimited power. Bukharin and twenty others were convicted in a show trial in March 1938. Eighteen faced a death sentence, including Bukharin, who sent Stalin a note, "Koba, why do you need me to die?"

Karl Radek was an Austrian writer and socialist agitator who worked with Lenin to organize the Bolsheviks and overthrow the Russian czar. A colorful, visible Communist personality both in and out of Russia, he was a favorite among Moscow journalists because of his cutting sense of humor and wild appearance. He fell into disfavor with Soviet leaders, though, and openly joined the Trotskyite network, which got him exiled to Siberia. He later renounced Trotsky, returned to Moscow and co-authored the new Soviet constitution in 1936. However, officials arrested him later that year for treason and sentenced him to prison through one of the public show trials. He is believed to have died in prison.

In April 1938, Alexei sent the family a telegram saying he would be home in June.

He sent another telegram in May saying he would meet them directly in Khvalynsk along the Volga for their summer vacation.

The summer passed with no word from him. Nina left Moscow to lead a Pioneers camp in the late summer.

She then returned home to learn of his arrest.

Nina Kosterina: A Young Communist in Stalinist Russia

> *The nightmare thought oppresses me day and night: is my father also an enemy? No, it cannot be, I don't believe it! It's all a terrible mistake! Mother is calm and steadfast. She tries to reassure us; she is forever going somewhere, writing to someone, and feels sure that the misunderstanding will soon be cleared up.*
>
> Nina's Diary, September 7, 1938

After the Party expelled Alexei, "he could not find any job," Nina's sister Elena recalled. "So he went to Kolyma to work there. He got fixed up in a job in the editorial office of a local newspaper. He wrote to mother and asked her to come with the junior daughter (Vera)."

Their mother took Vera and went to stay with Alexei in Kolyma. "Unexpectedly, people came to arrest him," Elena said. "An official of the local NKVD (People's Commissariat of

Interior Affairs) told mother to take her daughter and go away immediately. Mother did what he said. She came to Moscow, where all the relatives came to meet her. I did not know at that time that my father had been arrested. Mother wrote a letter to Stalin. She was not afraid of anything."

Nina feared and prepared herself for the worse in terms of the impact of her father's arrest on her Komsomol work.

She expected her unit to expel and shun her, yet her leader "consoled me and advised me to keep up my spirit, not to despair. I was assigned a Pioneer unit again, although I protested emphatically, pointing to my situation." When the unit elected new leaders, she expected to be disqualified and again reported with amazement that the unit actually elected her to one of the positions, even though it disqualified a fellow member in the same predicament.

This support—baffling even to Nina—certainly helped her to cope with the stress of the situation. Meanwhile, Nina's mother started looking for work, and Nina expressed fear about how they would make ends meet without Alexei's income.

In October 1938, when Nina was seventeen, the family received a letter from Uncle Ilya confirming he was in prison. Ilya was the father of Nina's cousin Stella. "Grandmother is upset, mama is angry and berates us as if we were to blame," Nina wrote. "She also rages at father ... And I have not a shadow of doubt that he is innocent."

Many months went by and then news came in March 1939 that Uncle Ilya had been freed. Nina struggled to understand the fearful behavior of the grownups around her. When she applied for admission to the Institute of Geology, she answered questions about her family connections honestly.

> *When I told them at home about my talk with the director, everybody flew into wild fits of hysterics: why did I talk about our relatives? Why did I mention my Communist aunts? I declared that I would never stoop to anything so vile as lying or concealment. And then everybody jumped on me—my aunts, mother, grandmother: "Brainless idiot! Hasn't learned how to live yet! Doesn't know that you must lie, that you must say 'I don't know'! My aunts are trembling for their hides, and I was nauseated listening to them. They want me to follow their example and try to make my way by 'accommodating myself'—to vileness! No, my Komsomol honor is much more precious to me than 'getting on.'*
>
> Nina's Diary, August 22, 1939

More than a year went by with no change in their situation. In November 1940, the family received a letter from Alexei reporting that a special secret police court pronounced him a "socially dangerous element" and gave him a five-year sentence in a gulag prison camp. He described the place where he would undergo "reeducation."

Nina marveled at the strength and freshness he displayed in the letter despite having been in prison for twenty-six months already awaiting his trial.

> *A wild canyon, a cold, crystalline, transparent, rapid forest stream. Papa was assigned as a work-team leader on a road-building project. His team consists of three former border guard lieutenants and two workers. All of them either 'dangerous elements' or 'active Trotskyites,' etc. Father wrote a beautiful description of the taiga*

(forest) and his comrades in misfortune. And he sent us a song composed in prison by a Moscow operetta singer.

Nina's Diary, November 30, 1940

The Russian Gulag

Gulag was an acronym for the Russian initials for Chief Administration of Corrective Labor Camps.

The gates of many gulag camps welcomed newcomers with the slogan: "Labour is a matter of honour, courage and heroism."

The Soviets created three types of gulags:

★ Factory or agricultural colonies

★ Camps for class-dangerous people to carry out mass work

★ Punitive camps that used strict isolation to hold people moved from other camps because they were considered the hardest to control

By 1937, thirty-five groups of camps already existed, most in Siberia. Each group contained about two hundred camps. Each camp had about twelve hundred prisoners.

Many prisoners did not survive the long, hard journeys to the gulags, and the camps themselves had high death rates.

Typical gulag work included harvesting lumber, building roads, railroads, canals, hydroelectric plants, and mining coal, copper and gold. Sixteen-hour work days were the rule.

Officials were strict about family access to the prisoners. Only relatives could send small packages every three months. In Leningrad, these could only be mailed from a post office about one hundred kilometers from the city, which meant relatives had to take a difficult ride in crowded trains to mail supplies to their loved ones.

No one knows the exact number of people who became gulag prisoners over the years. Estimates range from three to fifteen million.

Nina's family received another letter from Alexei on December 31, 1940, written a month earlier from his new gulag location.

He was reassigned to a drilling party studying terrain for bridge-building sites. He worked as a laborer, living in tents and traveling from river to river.

His letter was high-spirited, painting a vivid picture of the nature and people he encountered. He described the extreme cold and digging through thick snow to pitch their tents beside an unmapped river they were to study.

He responded to Anna's scolding for not trying harder to appeal his conviction: "There is nothing to be said about my case. There is no case, only an elephant out of a soap bubble. I cannot refute what is not, was not, and could never have been…"

This was the last communication from Alexei before the war and Nina's death at the war front.

An Empty Retreat

In 1939, the Soviet Central Committee issued a report admitting that many Communists had been wrongly accused during the 1937 and 1938 purges. The declaration meant little in real changes for most families. A large number of surviving Great Purge victims weren't released until after Nikita Khrushchev took over the Soviet leadership and openly talked about Stalin's crimes in 1956.

Stalin had Trotsky convicted from afar for treason, murder, conspiracy and espionage. While living in Mexico City in 1940, Trotsky was killed by an assassin believed to have been hired by Stalin.

What happened to two of Nina's uncles is confusing.

Uncle Misha apparently was arrested again at some point and executed, according to records the family found later. His wife, Anya, eventually emerged from prison camp.

Nina wrote in her diary that Uncle Ilya was released from prison, but the family was later informed by officials that he had been executed. Uncle Vasia died when his health deteriorated from the stress of his persecution.

Petro Grigorenko, a former Russian officer and good friend of Alexei's in the 1950s-1960s, wrote in his memoir that Alexei shared how his mother, herself a Bolshevik since 1917, suffered from the stress of her family's erosion.

"When her eldest son (Misha) was arrested, his mother put her own party card on the desk of the secretary of her party organization and declared that she was unable to remain a member of an organization that could permit such injustice," Grigorenko wrote. "After the death of her middle son (Vasia) and arrest of her younger son (Alexei), she too died."

Alexei, one of about six hundred writers sentenced to prisons or work camps, eventually emerged from the gulag and continued his work as a journalist. He spent seventeen years in work camps or exile.

All Soviet citizens were forced to choose between self-expression and self-preservation during the Stalin years. Their dilemma—choosing the safe route didn't necessarily keep a person or their family safe.

And, as Nina passionately expressed, choosing safety at the expense of honesty chipped away at one's dignity and self-pride.

Writers and artists such as Alexei faced an extra dilemma since their choice of ideas was expressed more publicly through their work.

Could they stay faithful to their art and faithful to their country at the same time? It was a delicate balance to achieve.

Pursuing a Passion for Art

I would die of wretchedness and boredom, or would become a drunkard, if it were not for poetry, for music and for my books . . .

Nina's Diary, March 2, 1941

Nina had an artistic soul. She craved art of all kinds and she was unapologetic in judging its quality and value to her life.

She filled her diary with details about authors, books, plays and music that captured her attention and shaped her thinking.

She was on a constant search for new ideas, new truths and an understanding of her world. She used art to feed this curiosity, drinking up anything she could consume.

Art always has held an important role in Russian life, and the desire by some Russian artists to break out of old traditions made them vital players in the revolution.

Many of these artists believed in the Bolshevik cause and did their part to create social changes. They experimented with new subjects and approaches while working to help advance the new society.

Art in Revolutionary Times

When the Bolsheviks gained power, they declared cultural activities important to the cause. They put new policies in place to give artists the chance to exhibit their works in the streets, theaters, clubs and museums.

New literary and cultural cadres formed within the worker population. These groups organized activities such as workshops devoted to literature, painting, theater and music. Agitational art, known as agit-prop, sprang up everywhere featuring large cartoon-like posters educating people on a variety of social issues such as hygiene and literacy.

Young groups of actors wrote and performed simple political skits in public gatherings and for Red Army troops.

New museums of contemporary art opened. Movie houses imported foreign films in large numbers, especially from Hollywood. Workers and peasants, dutifully expected to attend Bolshevik socialist lectures, preferred instead to see a Hollywood film and often waited in line for hours to do so.

And they enjoyed many U.S. and European authors translated into Russian during the 1920s, especially science fiction writers.

Some artists looked for ideas from America as another "new world" that had shaken off the oppression of an old monarchy, although their Communist goal was to exceed what the American capitalists had achieved.

Artists found new freedoms from the classical styles that had been taught for a long time in the Russian schools.

They experimented with approaches such as abstract modern art, impressionism, symbolism and Cubism. These styles used colors in bold new ways, relied on shapes and symbols more than realistic drawings, and made the viewer think harder to find meaning.

Some artists explored the relationship between man and machine.

Some experimented with textiles, ceramics and architecture to explore how art could serve the collective features of their new Communist society.

Some focused on creating monuments and sculptures.

Others focused on "socialist realism"—art that captured the everyday life of the peasants, revolutionaries, laborers and the Red Army.

Behind the flurry of artistic growth and excitement, debate raged among the new Soviet Union leaders. Should art from the old Russia be preserved and open to citizens, or should it be destroyed or hidden away to help with rapidly forming a new society? Should artists be allowed to contribute in their own way and challenge socialist beliefs if they wished, or should they create only works that helped the country's Marxist goals?

Leaders such as Trotsky supported the philosophies of avant-garde artists, who promoted modern views and scoffed at old traditions. They believed in rapidly constructing the new society. They used their art to shock people and stimulate action.

Lenin was not a fan of the newer art styles, saying he took no joy from them. He also wanted to preserve artifacts and traditions from czarist Russia to avoid alienating other artists who could help gradually construct a new society.

Yet the paths of Russian artists mirrored the lives of citizens. The 1920s promised more freedom of expression and hope for a strong future. This disappeared by the 1930s as old relationships and beliefs haunted artists under new restrictions. As with other citizens, some artists handled the pressure better than others.

Other artists just wanted the freedom to experiment; they bristled when the government tried to interfere with their work.

Alexei's Role in the Arts World

The politics of the art world influenced Nina perhaps more than she realized.

Her family's status in the community and living income depended on her father, Alexei, getting work as a writer.

Alexei contributed to the revolution as an artist and participated in the artistic revolution afterwards. His writings often fell into what became known as the socialist realism category. He published his works about Russian Civil War personalities in different reviews, almanacs and story collections.

When Stalin created unions that controlled all aspects of artists' lives, this directly impacted Alexei and his family. Nina last saw her father as the government sent him on a socialist realism mission to document life in the Russian Far East.

Growth of Socialist Realism

Censorship began in the mid-1920s. Soviet leaders cleansed most libraries of books not supporting their new philosophy and changed history books used in schools. A state committee started screening and banning certain films and theater plays that showed bourgeois ways or seemed too critical of the country's troubles.

Stalin involved himself in the arts after he took over the top leadership role in 1928. This prompted a cultural revolution from 1928 to 1932. He formed unions for each art discipline to control jobs, housing, supplies, exhibits, sales, and an artist's social status.

Stalin's government also declared socialist realism the only acceptable approach to art as the state tried to eliminate any lingering signs of capitalism in the country.

The guidelines were unclear about exactly what socialist realism was. It needed to be understood easily by the workers and peasants, popular with the masses and a good way to tell the Communist story.

A new constitution created for the writer's union tried to help its members by explaining that socialist realism "demands from the artist a true and historically concrete depiction of reality in its revolutionary development...combined with the task of educating workers in the spirit of Communism."

Paintings often used rich, earthy tones or simple line drawings done in pencil or charcoal to show citizens going about the tasks necessary to create a socialist society.

Writings featured the noble, courageous and heroic qualities of people facing challenges with a Bolshevik attitude. Artists joined brigades of workers in factories, on farms and on construction sites so they could document scenes celebrating the new way of life. Some painters received assignments to train Red

Army soldiers in how to express themselves visually.

Committees started to hire artists to produce specific works on specific subjects. This severely limited the artists' freedom to choose subjects and produce what they wanted if they were to earn a living under the new regime.

More and more, the assignments involved emphasizing the "collective" nature of socialist life. A good example is the painting *Collective Farm Youth Listening to the Radio*, commissioned to show a group of young people happily listening to a radio together instead of home alone in an anti-Communist manner.

Books and web sites now abound covering the early Russian avant-garde and Stalin period, with original works considered collector's items

Artists faced a serious predicament—express themselves within the official guidelines or suffer the consequences.

Stalin's purges touched many artists, including the avant-garde. They had shunned the old in favor of the new all along, but officials suddenly remembered their old association with Trotsky once he was exiled and accused of trying to overthrow Stalin.

The purges also caused practical problems, for visual artists especially. Works featuring people who suddenly disappeared in the wave of arrests needed changing to eliminate any depiction of those who had fallen from grace.

Nina's Favorite Authors

Several of Nina's favorite authors were part of this revolutionary era—authors such as Maxim Gorky, Vladimir Vladimirovich Mayakovsky and Alexander Alexandrovich Blok. She described these authors as "amicable tenants in a large apartment" living side by side in her mind.

A Russian stamp honoring Maxim Gorky

Gorky was a well-known writer often called the "founding father of soviet literature" because his works focused on social and political realities of the time. He was closely linked with Lenin, Trotsky and Stalin in helping the Bolsheviks gain power.

These connections earned him a place as the official cultural spokesman for the Communists, although his relationship with Lenin and the other leaders sometimes was rocky. Gorky even opened a publishing house to help intellectuals not directly tied to the Communist Party. Many of these writers believed that literature should not be influenced by any outside direction.

Gorky died just as Nina was beginning her diary and she described his death as a "personal sorrow" to her. "I love Gorky," Nina wrote, explaining how his socialist works inspired her. "I read him and reread him, and then read him again."

Moscow monument to Mayakovsky

Mayakovsky was a poet who experimented with futuristic ideas. He was involved in Moscow theater in the late 1920s as Nina's artistic tastes were developing. He used satire to fight against the increasing government censorship. This was considered anti-socialist and put him at odds with state officials. He committed suicide in 1930.

Blok was a lyrical poet who wrote simple, melodic poems sometimes recited to the accompaniment of a musical instrument. He portrayed a spiritually exhausted and disillusioned world in his works before the revolution, and he was among the first artists to declare their support for the new Bolshevik regime when it overthrew the royal government. Blok found energy in the revolutionary movement. He helped make posters with simple language and cartoons to educate the illiterate population about the benefits of the new regime, public health and safety at work.

Nina the Passionate Critic

Nina seemed less concerned about the political drama happening in the art world than the chance to experience art as a constant in her life. She was no doubt influenced in her early training on techniques, styles and philosophies by the involvement of her father and extended family in the arts community.

She described visiting the Museum of Modern Western Art three years after a family friend first took her there to explain the works in detail. She left the museum a second time still confused about what she saw. This frustrated her. She needed to understand the art she studied.

"Books, theatre, movies—my good companions in life," she wrote. "By hook or by crook, often at the risk of a row with the ushers, I get into theatres. Books I pick up at random, without plan or system. This often makes me feel that my 'brains are addled,' 'loaded with all sorts of trash.'"

She used her diary to organize facts, impressions and moods about the things she saw, heard or read. She joked about having little metal shelves with labels in her head as her "storage room." She enjoyed discovering new artists and works, then trying to understand what her tastes were.

Nina saw many films and plays, but books and music dominated her interests.

"Books remind me with particular sharpness that, essentially, I am only on the threshold of the huge and marvelous temple of science and art. Every step forward gives me much, but also opens horizons that leave me breathless," she wrote. Books sometimes moved her to tears and helped her through troubled times. She described relying on authors such as Heinrich Heine as emotional balm after her father's arrest, her initial rejection to college and her forced trip to Baku.

Heine, a German writer from the early 1800s, produced theatrical dramas, political satire and lyrical poetry. He used a witty and critical approach that often attacked religion and conservative politics, making him popular with European intellectuals and controversial at home, where he faced much ridicule and censorship. His ideas influenced some of the great thinkers of the century, including Karl Marx, whose socialist theories later transformed portions of the world such as Russia. Heine "went with me to Baku, he returned with me, and again he smiles to me sadly…" Nina wrote in describing his importance to her.

Nina showed her ability to go against the wave of popular opinion when she analyzed the works of Mikhail

Zoshchenko, a non-Marxist writer championed by Gorky. He was often compared with the famous American writer O. Henry, who helped make the short story a popular form in the early 1900s. Russians called O. Henry the American Zocshchenko as a way to suggest who they considered better. "That's silly, of course," Nina wrote with irritation. "O. Henry is incomparably better, deeper, more original, and—most importantly—more intelligent than Zoshchenko."

Nina visited Moscow's Lenin Library so often that the librarians knew her well and filled out her requests quickly, even saving books they knew she wanted for her next visit.

> *I love the reading room. A stern silence reigns here. Not a deadly, oppressive or anxiously watchful*

> *silence, but a silence of the mind, which disposes one to absorbed, thoughtful work. The rustling of pages as they are turned, the whisper of the librarians, the faint breeze that rises whenever anyone enters or leaves. The quiet of the reading room reminds me of the quiet of a wood on a windless day— it is so deep that you hear the beating of your own heart, yet all around you life seethes and pulses.*
>
> Nina's Diary, December 15, 1939

Music was Nina's other art passion where she invested much time documenting what she heard and liked. She enjoyed the Russian folk songs that often rang out in her home, school and Komsomol unit. She played the guitar—not very well, she believed—and apparently didn't have much of a singing voice.

But as with other art, she found her calling in the study of the classics and theory behind them.

She regularly attended the opera and concerts where orchestras covered the masters of classical music—Beethoven, Mozart, Mussorgsky, Bach, Tchaikovsky, Wagner and others. She read their biographies and studied up on musical theory so she could understand how the works were composed.

> *Why do I, a future geologist, need all this? It seems to me that one cannot be a cultured person without understanding music. That is one thing. And another is that I simply love music. As no other art, it carries me away to unknown regions, it brings me marvelous dreams and magical visions. In music there is movement, flight. Architecture, painting, sculpture are static, something split off from life and forever deadened . . . "*
>
> Nina's Diary, September 30, 1940

A Form of Nourishment

Artists create to inspire, inform, entertain, evoke emotion, provoke new thinking and help us make sense of our lives. Soviet artists persisted in their personal quests throughout the most challenging times of political purges and censorship, which lasted until the 1950s. Many served their country during the war by creating posters, battle paintings and other works to rally citizens in the fight against the Germans. They also documented the atrocities happening.

Even with the pro-Communist viewpoint, the requirement for socialist realism did at least produce many interesting works and capture slices of everyday life in the Soviet Union. And some Western art was still imported for citizens to enjoy.

Nina was an appreciative consumer. She needed art like she needed air and food. It enriched her life, inspired her and helped her sort through challenges and tough questions. In a way, it was her best friend—always available, usually reliable, open to being analyzed and never causing her heartache and grief as she experienced with the people in her life.

Juggling Friendships and Romance

Grisha used to say that I am beautiful. That boy idealized everything in me. How far all that is now...I remember our walks to the Moskva River. It was winter, a very harsh winter, but we strolled for hours along the deserted embankment, where it was, of course, especially cold. We kissed a lot toward the end. His kisses were shy, but passionate. And I never gave him an answering kiss. Why? I was embarrassed, it seemed funny and awkward.

Nina's Diary, November 16, 1940

A best friend, a stormy first love, a mentor, a Komsomol leader, a bothersome older man and a college lover—these were some of the people swirling in Nina's life as she became a young woman.

Nina's role as a Communist seemed to dominate her thinking and activities. Yet she had the same desire for friends and love held by people around the world. Relationships challenged her more than her one-way romance with art or her beloved Moscow. People didn't always behave the way she hoped. They were unpredictable, sometimes unreliable and often had different opinions. They filled her with joy and hope, and they made her ponder where her life was going.

Nina also fretted about her appearance. With dark hair and olive skin, she didn't like her Asiatic features and complained about "her homeliness and shabbiness, the obvious cheapness of my clothes. My dear relatives often tell me that I am homely. Thanks for the kindness, but I know it myself."

As a teen, her friendship with Lena Gershman and first romance with Grisha Grinblat (his formal first name was Grigori) became a stormy triangle of companionship spanning four years, with Grisha dating both girls at different points. Their emotions swirled, with the three exchanging sheets of deeply felt poetry and letters while opening their diaries for each other.

Grisha Grinblat

Nina, and sometimes Lena, sought advice from an older Communist mentor—Tatyana Alexdrandrova. The teacher spoke honestly and caringly to the girls about their lives. She challenged Nina to be a better person. Nina respected her for that.

Nina also enjoyed friendship and advice from a Komsomol unit leader named Nina Andreyevna.

And she displayed her no-nonsense courage when resisting repeated, unwanted sexual advances from an older writer. Later, she wrote joyously of meeting Sergei, a fellow college student she called Seryoga, at her geology summer camp in the days before the war and beginning a mature relationship.

Her friendships mattered to her. She struggled with loneliness and doubts when her friends were scattered by the early days of the war and couldn't help her sort through fears about becoming a soldier.

The Tight Knit Trio

When Nina started her diary in 1936 at the age of fifteen, she was beginning a new school and joining her Komsomol unit. A year later, Nina had met Lena and Grisha in the Komsomol and the three were working together on projects. Nina and Grisha began to flirt with each other.

The threesome took long walks together around Moscow, talking about things happening in their lives, sorting through their feelings or just wandering aimlessly. They had affectionate names for each other. Nina was "Ninok" to Lena and "Ninochka" to Grisha or apparently "Ninka" when feelings were less romantic. Lena was "Lenka" and Grisha was "Grishka."

Nina painted a picture of Grisha as a moody, romantic young man with intelligent blue eyes who wanted to become a scientist. He had dark, wavy hair and thick eyebrows that jutted into a strong V, giving him a serious expression. Nina described him as reciting poetry during conversations, struggling with sports and tending to brood. Grisha became jealous when Nina hung out with other boys, such as the time a boy was visiting her home to teach her to ride a bicycle.

    The threesome's friendship took a twist several months later, in April 1938, when Lena declared her love for Grisha and Grisha declared his love for Nina. At first, Nina didn't share his feelings but a few days later, she wrote, "Every day I become more and more convinced that the girl whom Grisha will love will be a lucky girl. Grisha's love ennobles a person."

Thus began a rollercoaster of emotions that lasted two years. Nina and Grisha went back and forth between joyous love, affectionate friendship and total exasperation with each other. Through it all, Lena weathered the storm as the constant friend, sometimes feeling left out and struggling with her own affections for Grisha. Nina thought Lena was very pretty, with black curls in her hair. Lena apparently had a hard time with her schoolwork, she faced conflict at home with her father, and she tended to get discouraged about her abilities.

As Nina and Grisha parted for the summer holiday just a few months into their romance, they said good-bye "like two people who love each other," she wrote. Yet they returned in September with their emotions cooled. They agreed just to be friends.

Grisha then revived his romance with Lena. He and Nina became more hostile with each other, but they couldn't stay apart. They spent all that autumn walking the streets of Moscow, exchanging notes and trying to sort through their feelings.

Nina's friendship grew stronger with Lena. She stressed out when Lena became secretive and she relished how they shared their feelings, relying on each other to make sense of their lives. "I am very fond of Lenka," she wrote. "I love her with a kind of special warmth. I cherish a secret hope that we'll be friends all our lives. I used to think we were very different, but now I think we are very much alike despite all differences."

By the spring of 1939, Nina and Grisha had declared their love for each other again, even though this put a strain on her friendship with Lena. "I am sorry for Lena. I am happy, and she is lonely," she wrote. "I am eighteen, I am loved, and I love! Beautiful!"

She expressed anger when Lena didn't respond to her letters over their summer break. "Not a line from Lena. I understand that things are difficult for her . . . But is that a way for a friend to behave? I must have a talk with her and try to help her."

The tension between the threesome reached a breaking point that fall as they quarreled and sniped with each other. By the winter of 1939, Nina worried that her romance with Grisha and friendship with Lena were over.

"I have lately begun to think more and more often of Grisha. And I regret the lost pure friendship and love," she wrote. "And Lena? I loved her very much and still do . . . How good it would be to meet as before, and talk and talk . . . But all the paths are overgrown with grass. . . "

Eight months then passed without Nina and Grisha being in touch.

Dealing With Her Emerging Sexuality

Nina stayed mainly within her small circle of friends. She was not overly interested in fashion and dating. But becoming a young woman still brought excitement and confusion.

She loved to dance and have fun at activities happening with her school and Communist groups. She battled a period of intense jealousy about another girl and wrote critical words about girls trying to get attention with their revealing clothes and behaviors. She struggled with her own emerging feelings of sexuality and wondered how to handle attention from boys and older men.

She attracted some unwanted admiration. First, one of her teachers, a middle-aged Communist Party member, kept asking her on dates. Then she had a series of encounters with a writer she called Fishberg. He repeatedly telephoned her, groped her at events and badgered her to spend time with him. In a moment when she was feeling low about herself, she accepted an invitation to his apartment and immediately regretted it.

> I came, took off my coat, and sat down on the sofa—a vile, shabby, creaky sofa. It smelled of dust and mold and bedbugs. He sat down near me and began to read Mayakovsky's poems, and his own. He read badly, in a silly singsong. I felt nauseated. And he, who considers himself a poet, didn't have the slightest idea of what was happening inside me. This jellyfish tried to embrace and kiss me. I pushed him away violently, with all

my strength (and I seem to have inherited my father's strength), put on my coat and left . . .

Nina's Diary, April 13, 1938

Luckily, Nina didn't suffer too greatly from these situations. This wasn't always the case for young women in the new regime.

The Communists promised new freedoms and rights to be enjoyed by women, but the realities of liberation suggested a complicated picture.

Casual sex outside of marriage became a popular philosophy as part of the rebellion against old traditions. Some teenage girls and women liked the new sense of freedom from oppressive traditions about marriage and their duties. Others felt pressured to participate in a lifestyle they didn't want.

The dilemma was serious. To resist such attention, especially from party officials or those in some position of power, could suggest a girl was bourgeoisie and not a true Communist. It could impact her job and education choices, or those of her family. But going along with such sexual contact carried a host of problems as well.

Nina was disgusted with the idea of older men pursuing younger girls. She spared no harsh words for them in her conversations with Lena about the issue.

Then she experienced a confusing new set of emotions when she became infatuated with Lena's brother. He was twenty years older, married and showed no interest in her at all.

"I had almost no conversation with him, except for an exchange of a few insignificant phrases," Nina wrote of an encounter. "I spent a marvelous day and left in the evening, but . . . I left my heart there."

In the strained moments of their friendship, Lena taunted Nina about the crush and even Grisha suggested it was a reason he had cooled in his feelings for her. Within a month, her infatuation with Lena's older brother had faded away and Nina turned her attention back to Grisha.

Nina as a young woman of 18 with younger sister Elena

Nina also described a time when she became extremely jealous of another girl who was popular in her class and always had a crowd around her. Nina and another girl she described as a fellow "lonely and unhappy soul" concocted a plan to embarrass the popular girl and "create a circle of admirers around ourselves." Before they could carry out their plan, Nina stopped herself, realizing she had let envy get the best of her.

She described the evening as a powerful turning point in her sense of satisfaction with herself. She promised to stay on a more honest path as a human being and felt instantly happier.

Mentorship, Marxist Style

As a teen, Nina took comfort from friendships with two older

Komsomol leaders, Tatyana Alexandrovna and Nina Andreyevna.

Nina admired both women for their courage and wisdom. She sought their advice and welcomed their views about her strengths and weaknesses.

Tatyana was a teacher in charge of Nina's brigade of Komsomol and Young Pioneers units. Nina, Lena and Grisha often visited Tatyana at her apartment. She talked straight with them about their Communist duties and the need to rise above the petty behaviors of others.

After Nina's Uncle Misha and Aunt Anya were arrested, Nina visited Tatyana to share the story. She worried for her cousin Irma, sent off to an orphanage by the state police. Tatyana gave Nina money to help Irma, despite evidence that she was heading into her own troubled waters as the political purges spread. "People like Tatyana Alexandrovna are very rare and must be appreciated and treasured!" Nina wrote. "Poor woman, she looks bad now . . . She warned us recently to cut down our contacts with her, or we would get into difficulties with the director . . . But no one will ever make me turn away from Tatyana Alexandrovna, no matter what happens."

Nina's references to Tatyana in her diary stopped after October 1938.

Nina also found inspiration from Nina Andreyevna. They didn't see each other often, but Nina greatly enjoyed their encounters. She described feeling like she had "taken a cold, refreshing shower" after one visit to the older Nina. "She spoke to me frankly: one of my faults is lack of sensitivity to people; I try to make everyone fit my demands without considering the person's individual capacities and character."

When the older Nina's husband was arrested and she was forced from her job, she prepared to leave Moscow and start over in a new town. Nina mourned the loss of "the last friend of my youth."

Nina was especially touched when her friend sent a book written by Lenin as a farewell gift and added the following inscription:

> "To Nina, with the heartfelt wish that she will always preserve her directness and sincerity and rid herself of her supercilious contempt for people of lower intellectual development and of her mood of pessimism and passivity, which transforms the militant and active Nina into a benumbed 'sleeping beauty' with a certain tendency to whimpering and loss of perspective."

College Romance

Nina began more mature relationships when she started college. She had a short affair with a man named Zhorka. She described their meetings in her diary in third person, as if they were characters in a romance novel.

Later, she found love with the chief of the summer geology expedition, a fellow student named Sergei Nikitich, while they were away from the city for the summer. "There has been a tremendous change in my life," she wrote. "I am no longer 'alone and on my own,' I am 'someone else's.' It seems that my independence is over, that I will not be able any more to break away so easily, should it become necessary. The thread that binds me to this man is too strong."

She wrote of urgently wanting to retreat to Moscow so she could have thinking time to get clear about her feelings for him. She reflected on how easily people come together when away from their true surroundings.

"I know that I love him physically," she wrote. "But intellectually? Only Moscow can help me determine. This does not mean he must be a model of high intellect. But he must answer my inner needs. I must feel that he is a man who understands my thoughts and emotions . . ."

Nina's fifteen-year-old sister Elena accompanied her on the geology expedition.

"It was very beautiful there. Forest, openings, pines, raspberries, mushrooms, berries," Elena recalled. "We lived in an izba, a peasant's log hut . . . We did not know when the war started. There was no radio there."

Nina at a geology camp in 1941 right before Germany invaded Russia

Elena recalled the moment when they learned what was happening.

"We were at home in the village. At about noon, Sergei Nikitich came in. In fact, he almost rushed into the house and cried, 'Girls, the war!' We opened our mouths and fell silent. Nina stood rigid, with a changed countenance," Elena said. "Nina demanded to let her go. Sergei Nikitich did not want it. Nevertheless, Nina left us all the same."

Nina wrote Lena from her geology camp as the war began. She mentioned her new romance with Sergei but complained that she couldn't share everything about herself with him because he worried too much about her.

Workers were evacuating from Moscow and the city was closed. Civilians were told not to return. Elena's memory of what happened differs from what Nina wrote in her diary. Nina wrote that she left while Sergei was gone from their camp, leaving him a short note, "Don't feel sad, forget me and farewell."

Elena said that Sergei did not want Nina to leave, but he did get to say good-bye.

"Nina rushed about. She had to go to Moscow and she decided to go there alone. Sergei Nikitich and me went to see her off. I still remember that beautiful forest, leaves lighted up by the setting sun and the road through the forest," Elena said.

Nina stopped the two halfway to her destination several miles from the village of Morshansk. She said good-bye and continued her walking journey. "We stayed and saw her going. It was the last time I saw her," Elena said.

Later, she heard through friends and Nina's diary that Nina succeeded in hopping a train to Moscow with Russian soldiers, who hid her away from their commander.

When Nina reached Moscow, she discovered that Grisha had volunteered and been sent to war. "How I would like to be there with him, shoulder to shoulder," she wrote.

She described scribbling the threesome's names—Nina, Grisha, Lena—in the dust on furniture in her family's abandoned apartment and then feeling "terrified—gooseflesh over my body—of the silence, and that writing in the dust. I quickly wiped off the words and went out into the street . . ."

Meanwhile, Sergei sent an emotional letter to Moscow begging her to reconsider and return to the country right away.

"Rashness at this moment is tantamount to death . . ." he wrote. "I urge you, if it's not too late: take the first train going to Gorky, and come to the Urals. You must, after all, have some regard for your friends and family."

Nina did not reconsider, instead reflecting in her diary: "Yes, it was a marvelous summer, full of tender caresses, love, forest fairy tales, and promises 'until the grave' . . . I must go where my homeland calls me . . ."

The war eventually called Sergei as well, after he had delivered Elena and other students to evacuation sites, Elena said. He continued to think of Nina. While stationed with Russian troops in Berlin, Germany, he left an inscription on a wall: "Nina + Serezha."

Alone in the End

By the early days of the war, Nina had changed from a vivacious schoolgirl to a brooding twenty-year-old woman separated from all who mattered to her.

> *Oh, no, I am not flinty, not even hard as stone. And this is why it is so difficult for me now. There is no one around, and I am spending my last days here. Do you think that I am not tempted by all sorts of slippery thoughts, that I am not reluctant to leave my comfortable rooms and face the unknown? Oh-h, it isn't so, it isn't so at all...I feel so lonely, I need my friends so badly these last days...*
>
> Nina's Diary, November 14, 1941

Nina was already gone when a letter from Lena reached Nina's mother.

> *... I sent her three letters, but there is no answer. I am terribly worried. You know Nina's character. We, her friends, were always a little afraid of her flare-ups and out-bursts. I am afraid that, with her hot head, she*

> *will think up something wild. Keep her from doing anything reckless and let me know her address...Tell her the sad news: Grisha, our mutual friend, with whom we studied together for several years, was killed at the front . . .*
>
> Lena's Letter, December 28, 1941

It would have boosted Nina's spirits to know Lena was alive and still cared about her. She most likely never learned of Grisha's fate.

After the war, confusion surfaced about whether a different Grisha died in 1941 and this Grisha died in 1942. It is clear that he perished sometime during the first several months of the war.

Nina's time was over for parties, studying, long strolls around Moscow and tricky walks through the minefield of love and friendship.

She was off on a new mission, where her years of Marxist training probably was the best friend she had to cope with life as a guerrilla soldier in the brutal war unfolding around her.

Transforming from Student to Soldier

Do you remember, Nina Alexeyevna, how you secretly dreamed of experiencing great and stirring events, how you dreamed of storms and dangers? There—you have it—war! A predatory black beast has suddenly swooped down from behind dark clouds on our homeland. Well, I am ready...I want action, I want to go to the front . . .

Nina's Diary, June 23, 1941

At 3:15 a.m. on June 22, 1941, life changed dramatically for Soviet citizens. Millions of German soldiers in tanks, fighter planes and on foot launched a surprise "blitzkrieg" invasion of Russia's border with Poland. It sent the country into a deadly state of chaos.

"I'm being fired upon. What shall I do?" a Russian commander frantically radioed to headquarters. His superior officer, stationed miles away from the nightmare unfolding, radioed back, "You must be insane! No one is firing at you."

It took four hours before Stalin let his troops fire back. Aroused from sleep back in Moscow, he couldn't believe German dictator Adolph Hitler attacked without a formal declaration of war. Germany had already invaded other countries, but Stalin and Hitler even agreed to divide Poland and not attack each other. The Soviets supplied grain and war materials to Germany up to an hour before the invasion, unaware that the Germans were secretly waiting orders to invade.

Within five days, the Germans had taken 300,000 Russian prisoners and moved 150 miles deep into the country. They began fanning out to conquer major cities and seaports. Hitler planned to turn the vast Russian land into a "superstate" of living space for his superior race of Germans. "Everything I undertake is directed against the Russians," Hitler said. "If the West is too stupid or blind to grasp this, then I shall be compelled to come to an agreement with the Russians, beat the West, and then after their defeat, turn against the Soviet Union with all my forces."

The early days of the war looked impossible to reverse. Stalin's political purges had already claimed about 35,000 professional soldiers. The remaining Red Army was undersupplied and unprepared. Stalin's leaders began organizing new army recruits to help drive back the Germans. Millions of people quickly changed from students or laborers to soldiers and fighter pilots. This included about 95,000 young Komsomol members who joined the defenses in the early months of the war.

Nina was to be among them. When she returned to volunteer, she

Reproduction of a 1941 war recruiting poster — "Your Motherland Needs You!" — common at the time

learned her family was all gone and her beloved city being bombarded.

> *I came to Moscow October 24th, and was badly shaken by my first impressions. It began with our apartment—I found none of the family there. An empty house. I walked, utterly lost, from room to room...Outwardly, Moscow is the same, although the boarded-up windows in many houses jar the nerves. In some buildings, the doors and windows seem to have been forced out. A bomb struck the Moscow State University building...barricades are rising at intervals. Their fronts bristle with heavy rails, slanting forward. Antitank 'hedgehogs' stand in rows, and behind them, walls of sandbags with openings for guns...How my heart aches for everything in Moscow...I walk through the streets and think with terror: another ton of explosives, and this magnificent building will disappear . . .*

Nina's Diary, October 28, 1941

Nina's mother and youngest sister, Vera, evacuated to the Urals. People "were evacuated together with the institutions where they worked," said Nina's sister Elena. "Mother went to Kizil with the coal industry institution."

Elena, her cousin Stella and their aunt Katia were stationed with Nina at the geology camp when the Germans invaded. Katia, a geologist, was responsible for the expedition. Elena, Stella and Katia evacuated to a settlement in Novo-Troitsk while Nina returned to Moscow. Later, Elena said, the three relocated to the Saratov region. Then a new order came that sent Katia back to Moscow while sending Elena and Stella to Tiumen, where they reunited with Elena's mother, sister and grandmother. Daily living was tough, Elena reported, but the girls also continued with schooling and enjoyed social activities such as dances. They saw many young soldiers off to the war front.

Nina listened on the radio as Stalin rallied citizens to fight during that year's celebration of the Bolshevik revolution:

"If they want a war of extermination, they shall have it!" Stalin exclaimed while German and Russian guns rumbled in the distance and Soviet fighter aircraft patrolled overhead. "Our task now will be to destroy every German, to the very last man! Death to the German invaders!"

Mobilizing the Partisans

The war produced different kinds of partisans, a word used to describe supporters of the Soviet cause.

Some were militant peasant groups resisting the Germans. Soviet authorities loosely organized others into guerrilla bands that worked separate from the Red Army. And other partisans acted by themselves.

Russian propaganda portrayed partisans as the heroes of resistance struggles. Yet the reality was that the war—like all wars—produced many reluctant warriors. Once again, Soviet citizens faced no easy choices.

The government evacuated millions of workers, along with factory machines and equipment, to the regions farthest from the invading Germans—the Ural Mountains, Kazakhstan and Siberia. Trains and trucks carried people and equipment whenever possible, but many citizens suffered through long, exhausting marches on foot to these war-time hideouts.

Other citizens did not evacuate but stayed behind to defend their cities. They received scant instruction. Basic training in Leningrad, for example, took about sixteen hours.

Young Soviet women flooded officials with requests to fight at the front, especially at the beginning of the war.

Their motivations ranged from patriotism and a sense of duty to survival, hatred or revenge. Some ended up in partisan units after fleeing into the woods to escape Germans rounding up Russian workers for German factories. Some got caught up in the idea of romantic adventure. Some wanted a chance to start over and remove the stigma haunting their families during Stalin's political purges.

And toward the end of the war, some girls who had worked or lived with the Germans during the Russian occupation joined the partisans out of fear they would be called traitors. Soviet leaflets, newspapers and word of mouth messages made it brutally clear how traitors would be handled.

A Volunteer Soldier

Nina, at least, chose her warrior role and felt prepared through her years of Komsomol training. When the fear of war began looming a year earlier and Komsomol members trained to fight, Nina dove into the task with enthusiasm.

> *Red Army Day was, in a way, the climax and reward for my Komsomol work this past winter. The District Committee of the Komsomol arranged a militarized march from Moscow to Skhodnya to Nakhabino and back to Moscow as a test of the defense preparedness of the Komsomol. I was appointed company commander—my company consisted of the students*

Nina Kosterina: A Young Communist in Stalinist Russia

> *of our Institute. The test mobilization and march were a success. My company completed the march as scheduled; discipline and political work during the march were in strict conformity with orders from the command. I received a citation in the battalion orders. If war comes, I am ready for it . . .*
>
> Nina's Diary, February 24, 1940

Nina actually confided to her diary of a bigger fear than the dangers of war. She was near-sighted and couldn't shoot well. The army would discover this, she fretted, and toss her out. Still, she passed an initial exam and then made the final cut.

Even Nina's cousin, Irma, who was sent to an orphanage when Stalin's regime arrested her parents, volunteered as a Red Army soldier. She finished the war in Romania as a communications sergeant.

Nina seemed motivated to volunteer by a mixture of things. She had a strong sense of patriotism and hoped her action would help save her imprisoned father from his political troubles. Yet, she also had a quest for adventure.

"They say we'll have to parachute down," Nina wrote. "That's the easiest thing of all. We shall act singly, at best in pairs. This is the worst of it . . . In the woods, in snow, in the dark of the night, behind enemy lines."

While she waited for her deployment, Nina described the daily scene as the city tried to hold off the Germans. Air raid sirens screamed out regularly. People used earplugs to stifle the shattering noise level of bombs and anti-aircraft guns. Searchlights glided over the night sky and tracer bullets "spun long green threads across the sky." Casualties happened daily as bombs surprised people standing in line for food, traveling across the city or seeking shelter in their homes.

Lenin's body was moved from his Red Square tomb to Siberia. Stalin equipped an airplane for a quick getaway. The Metro subway became a command station bunker. Nina met this wartime reality with a combination of shock and anger, writing that she walked the streets freely even during the air raids and refused to wear earplugs or hide her head under a pillow.

Moscow citizens hung out red flags and prepared for the annual Bolshevik celebration. Stalin worked to rally everyone during a radio speech. He made the speech from the subway station since the usual location—the Bolshoi Theatre—now had a large bomb crater. He inflated the number of Germans lost so far in the war and downplayed Soviet soldier deaths.

> *And so, this is the day when Hitler promised to review his troops on Red Square. But everything turned out somewhat differently. Yesterday, Stalin addressed us. We all sat motionless by our receivers, listening to the leader's speech. And outside the windows, bombs were crashing—it was so extraordinary, so strange. Stalin's voice sounded calm, confident, without breaking for a moment. In the hall where he spoke, everyone shouted hurrah and greetings to him. Everything was the same as in the past, except for the booming artillery, which spoke of the extraordinary character of our time.*
>
> Nina's Diary, November 7, 1941

Nine days later, Nina left for the front.

The Komsomol's Central Committee assigned Nina to a guerrilla band stationed south of Moscow in an area occupied by the Germans. This made Nina a partizanka, the word to describe the war's Soviet partisan heroines.

When Nina parachuted behind enemy lines in November 1941, she entered a thorny world of life-or-death rules, mixed treatment of women as soldiers, rough camp life and friendships that were intense but fleeting as soldiers moved around or died.

Life as a Partizanka

Women represented only a small percentage of the Soviet partisans during World War II, and even fewer went behind enemy lines.

Documentaries, fiction and history textbooks painted the lives of the female partizankas lives as mythical struggles. These partisan heroines became inspirational examples of the "ideal"

Soviet girl and proof of how Soviet women had been liberated.

The truth revealed a more complicated picture when it came to their experiences, successes and struggles.

Partisan soldiers—men and women—were the "kamikazes" of the Soviet war effort, attacking and harassing the Germans in the territories they now occupied, usually through stealthy night raids.

Partisans worked as explosive experts, nurses, radio operators, scouts, information gatherers and liaisons with the local villagers.

Stalin's regime expected both Red Army and partisan soldiers to die rather than surrender to the Germans or desert their units. If they broke the oath, they understood that their comrades were to kill them.

Stalin outlined this "Not a Step Back" rule in an order distributed to all fighting units. After the war, Soviet authorities forbade publishing any details about the rule for forty years.

The Soviet propaganda about equal rights for women sat bitterly with many partizankas.

Some women served as fighters, scouts and spies. Others had kitchen and domestic duties. Still others ended up as girlfriends of Army officers, either out of pressure or because it was safer and came with more privileges.

Gaining trust and respect among the male soldiers took persistence, skill and savvy. Many women faced sexual harassment, abuse, neglect and sometimes rape. They were not spared the worst violence of the war.

When the Central Committee convened a conference of partizankas to see what challenges they were facing, the group complained about being forced into traditional domestic duties instead of training with weapons or participating in true partisan military duties. Even those who did often were expected to do both—fight and work in the kitchen and laundry.

Only a small number really carried out the partizanka feats highlighted in the literature and films celebrating their existence.

"Partisan girls often found themselves in a no-win situation," wrote historian Juliane Furst. "On the one hand, they were often denied permission to go and fight, while, on the other hand, any other work that they performed was not deemed to be sufficient for recognition."

Party officials tried to correct the situation, but life in partisan camps depended heavily on the beliefs and approach of the commanders. These men brought their own attitudes about women to the job. They decided how much law and order to enforce in the topsy turvey wartime environment. Some could not reconcile traditional views with women as fighters. Some considered the women a burden and untrustworthy. Others embraced the women as soldiers.

Nina's letters to her family were so limited that it is hard to know much about what she experienced and what assignments she faced. She was very athletic, skilled in outdoor living, strong-willed and not one to put up easily with much harassment from men.

Her first letter to her mother suggests she participated in scouting expeditions with her unit, detachment 9903.

> *"I have just returned from a mission, and am resting now. Soon I shall go again. I would like you to see how they outfitted us! Warm underwear, felt boots, woolen vests, mittens . . . In short, there is no danger of freezing. In the place where I live there are many young people . . . I had a sore throat from sleeping on the snow in the woods, but now I am well."*
>
> Nina's letter to her mother, December 8, 1941

It is likely that Nina appreciated the Komsomol's expectation that members be a positive influence in their units. Komsomol youth were supposed to attract new members, pay attention to the soldiers' political education and keep the young soldiers behaving according to party rule. Accounts gathered after the war show that some Komsomol members found this challenging. The living conditions were harsh and many young partisans had an attitude that strict rules no longer mattered because death was inevitable.

More partisans did join the Communist Party and Komsomol, though. Patriotic anger against the Germans played a part, and carrying a membership card became a status symbol since it automatically put the person in more danger. The card signaled that the soldiers were willing to die for their country.

An Early Casualty

Nina worked as a partizanka for about a month, during sub-zero blizzards while the Red Army launched a counterattack to drive the Germans back from Moscow. She probably didn't know the war was at a crucial point. The Soviets regained some control, and Hitler became preoccupied as Japan attacked the United States and the war became a global affair.

Nina's family received a second short but cheery letter from Nina in December. Then, an Army letter dated January 20, 1942, arrived:

> "Notice No. 54. Your daughter, Nina Alexeyevna Kosterina, native of Moscow, died in December 1941, in the fight for our Socialist Homeland. Faithful to her military oath, she showed heroism and courage in the performance of her duty."

No details about her death were offered at the time.

"Most deaths went unnoticed, especially those of girls who did not die with defiant words on their lips," historian

Juliane Furst wrote. "Sooner or later, most girls found themselves in a hopeless situation and became victims of the fact that, in most instances of direct combat, the Germans outnumbered their partisan opponents."

After the war, the government assembled a series of memory books about soldiers who died. One of the books includes a report about Nina's last mission. The family received a copy of this official report many years later from one of Nina's partisan colleagues.

In the report, a member of the unit described how a band of twenty-two partisans—Nina among them—departed on a mission December 19. They slipped behind enemy lines south of Moscow near the cities of Podolsk and Narofominsk. As they went deep into the woods, they fell into a German ambush, tripping a wire that set off an explosion. Fifteen partisans, including Nina, perished. The surviving seven ended their mission and returned to their base camp to report the attack. The goal of their mission was not shared.

The war continued through 1945.

German soldiers came to respect the stubborn courage of the Russians soldiers. They also came to dread what they called the Eastern front where the German and Soviet defense lines met. About eighty percent of Germany's war casualties happened here.

Hitler's quest for Soviet territory failed. Instead, Soviet soldiers raised their flag over Berlin as the war approached its end.

Nina's city and family survived the war even though she did not.

Moscow became a frustrating symbol of Russian persistence for the

Germans. Bombs and shells destroyed fewer than 350 buildings, falling way short of Hitler's vision to level the city. The Germans never made it to Red Square and the city did rise again like a phoenix, as Nina hoped.

Millions of people in several countries died in the global conflict. The losses were staggering and overwhelming. Yet behind each death was a string of personal stories woven together by a network of family and friends. Nina's story was among them.

Elena said the "sister-soldier" who shared the report about Nina's mission later helped by re-typing Nina's diary. "She then told how she met with brothers-soldiers, read it and cried. Everything was so familiar," Elena said.

Ovidi Gorchakov, a Russian author who wrote about Soviet military scouts and World War II operations, reported trying for many years to learn more details about Nina's last mission, even publishing an article asking witnesses to contact him. He succeeded only in finding out that Nina was considered missing at first until a fellow soldier came forward to report that Nina had died during the mission. Officials used this information to issue a death certificate to her family.

Many years later, when Nina's father published an afterword with her diary, he provided a few details about her early childhood and wrote simply of his pride for his daughter.

He didn't write of that bitter winter in 1942 when the world looked like it was falling apart and he learned, from his prison site in Kolyma, of his first daughter's death.

He didn't describe reading her diary after the war to learn that she proudly followed in her father's partisan footsteps in hopes of saving him from Stalin's purges. Even though he decided to make her story available to the world, there were some things he kept to himself.

Instead, Alexei ended his summary of Nina's life with the following thoughts:

> Many, after reading the diary, will say that in her life and death there is nothing exceptional. This is true. There were a lot of young women and men no less gifted who also gave up their lives for their homeland, for the future, for the cause of their fathers' and grandfathers'. There were millions of them. And in this we are fortunate. If this were not so, if such as Nina were the exception, our homeland could not have crushed fascism, and after the war would not have become so mighty. Happy is the nation that has such children.
>
> Alexei Kosterin, afterword in Russian version of Nina's diary, 1964

Rebuilding After the War

I do not remember if the war was already finished or not. We returned from evacuation. Mama returned earlier. There was a wardrobe in the room. I got into it for something and found a bundle. I saw Nina's belongings there. I opened the bundle and thought that Mama still was waiting for Nina. When I unbound it, I saw a notebook, opened it and understood it was a diary. My heart snk, everything turned upside down. I got frightened. 'My God, Ninka...' I thought that I should hide it again...

Elena Kosterina, 2004 Interview

The country was in tatters. As the Soviets slowly began driving the Germans out and more regions became safe, Nina's family returned to their Moscow apartment in

1943 to begin rebuilding the Kosterin lives. They were surrounded by millions of other citizens doing the same.

Families, cities, villages, roads and more—rebuilding became the new focus. Homes, roads and factories needed repair. People needed food and basic supplies. Millions needed information about the fate of loved ones. Physical and emotional wounds needed healing.

And all was to be done under Joseph Stalin's iron fist.

Stalin's Final Decade

Stalin emerged the victor over Adolph Hitler, yet his survey of the war's devastation quickly turned him to the new priority of repairing the damage. Russian losses included 70,000 villages, 1,700 towns, 32,000 factories, 40,000 miles of railroad tracks and 25 million people homeless. Millions had been wounded or killed in the conflict, and millions more died of starvation.

The hard work of the 1920s and 1930s to develop the country's agriculture and industry was lost.

Stalin quickly rebuilt his political control and dashed hopes that the war somehow changed his level of fear and paranoia against his own people. He had eased some restrictions during the war to help boost the level of patriotism. Afterwards, he quickly put all rules back into place and began more purges.

Stalin's suspicions even included Western countries that had been allies during the war. He worked to create a land buffer between Europe and Russia by trying to take more of Germany's land, ordering Soviet occupations of Hungary, Romania, Greece, Poland and Bulgaria, and giving war supplies to the Communist Chinese. Fear rose in democratic countries about Communism spreading out and taking control over the world.

This period became known as the Cold War, when tension between Western countries and the Soviet Union kept relationships just short of a real war.

Getting Back on Track

Nina's mother, Anna, got work as a secretary at a coal institution. "She was efficient, honest, very diligent, painstaking," recalled Elena. "She had a good memory. She knew all of the orders by heart. If something happened, everybody went to Anna Mikhailovna for help."

Elena and Nina's other sister, Vera, returned to school.

Elena said Nina's diary, written in four copybooks, had one brief outing in the immediate post-war years.

> *Later on I found out that Mama had read the diaries and took them to show Serafimovich (an editor). He read them, too, and gave a high appreciation to them as a good writer's work. He said that if it was another time, he would publish it.*
> Elena Kosterina, 2004 Interview

The Soviets finally allowed Nina's father to return to Moscow in 1955. He apparently remained under suspicion by Stalin's regime even then.

"As soon as he came to Moscow, the militia officer appeared," Elena recalled. "The father rushed about at the end of his tether. He explained that he arrived to Moscow to see his children. Mama worried very much. Fortunately, he was not arrested that time. He went away. I was summoned for several times to be interrogated concerning the father. Once I told them sharply: 'You ought to be ashamed! The father did not see his children for eleven years.'"

Alexei Kosterin in 1946 or 1947

Elena said the police forced Alexei to leave Moscow. He took Nina's diaries with him and went to a village where he found a job and got involved in local community activities. The authorities did not like his involvement, Elena said, so someone knocked on his window one night and told him to leave or face arrest the next day. He fled the village across a frozen river.

"Supposedly he often carried the diaries by him and he had them by him when he had to escape from the village," Elena said. "It was when he escaped in the night, fell in the ice hole. That time, he wetted the diaries slightly."

Alexei landed in the city of Saratov and found a job with an oil pipeline crew. The police forbade him from returning to Moscow. "Mama wrote to him: 'I wish you to find a wife.' She wanted him to arrange his fate where he lived," Elena said.

By now, Elena was grown, had finished her schooling and was pursuing a lifelong interest in insects and plants. She got a job in Minsk checking crops. She became involved in the Komsomol, married, returned to Moscow and worked as an inspector entomologist. Elena gave birth to a son, Alexey. Her husband worked in construction but he served two years in prison, accused of stealing construction materials. He and Elena divorced after his release.

Alexei got involved in the local theater and met a woman, Vera Ivanovna, who did become his second wife. "It affected our mother very much in spite of the fact that she offered this way out herself," Elena said. Later, when Elena's young son became very ill and the family was struggling to make ends meet in Moscow, Alexei and his new wife offered to care for the child for a summer and nurse him back to health. This plan worked and young Alexey regained his strength.

During this time, Elena bumped into Nina's old school friend, Lena, in Moscow. "As I remember, I got a tram and saw Lena there," Elena said. "'Is it you, Lena?' I asked. She got confused. 'Why don't you come to us?' She answered, 'I am ashamed! Nina and Grisha have perished, and I have stayed alive. I cannot.'"

Lena Gershman years later in Moscow in 1987

Anna invited Lena to her apartment and she did finally come. "She looked through the diary and said in spite of what was written, Grisha was attracted to her. She loved him very much," Elena said. Lena also pecked out her own manuscript about Nina and their friendship on a typewriter.

A Bumpy Path to Openness

Stalin died in 1953. The new USSR leader, Nikita Khrushchev, stunned the world by denouncing Stalin in what started as a secret speech to the Soviet congress in 1956. He presented a report outlining many of the horrors from the Stalin regime. He criticized Stalin for allowing his government to lose sight of the party principles, and he promised to heal all wounds.

Information played an interesting role in Soviet life. The government collected a dizzying amount of data about the country's industries, agriculture, geography, political system—and its citizens. Secret police used detailed information about individuals and their families as a key weapon to terrorize the population.

Yet information also was tightly controlled for decades. Russian citizens rarely had access to unedited facts about events in their country or elsewhere in the world.

When Khrushchev started lifting information restrictions a bit, he may not have permitted much freedom in information about current Soviet activities but he allowed citizens to start sharing their stories from the 1920s and 1930s.

When the government loosened censorship slightly in the 1960s, stories emerged in the form of memoirs, letters, diaries and personal accounts. Nina's family believed the "different time" described by the editor so many years earlier had finally arrived.

They offered her diary to the Soviet monthly literary magazine, Novy Mir. In December 1962, the magazine published it as *The Diary*. In 1964, a publishing house released it as a Russian book titled *The Diary of Nina Kosterina*.

The book's forward highlighted Nina's passionate spirit and strong ideals.

> *You will delight in getting to know a person who is inquisitive, active, passionately in love with life, avidly peering with sharp eyes at the world and knowing how to see it in all its sunny and unbounded expanse. How much Nina reads— the names of writers and books literally fill many pages of her diary! How avidly she acquaints herself with everything that makes genuine art, whether it be a new show at the theatre, a film, a painting in the Tretyakovsky Gallery or a symphonic concert! How she knows how to feel the beauty of nature! . . .*

> *Before you, at first, is a straightforward kid, and then a young woman, alive, thoughtful, energetic, full to the brim with aspiration for the beautiful, firmly believing in the unshakable rightness of that great cause that shapes our people...Nina makes high demands. She lives without allowances, she does not permit herself to indulgence in anything, applying the same standards to everything in the world.*
>
> Russian Children's Author Lev Kassil, foreword in 1964 Russian version of Nina's diary

During this period, Alexei was allowed to return to Moscow and regain his membership in the Communist Party and the Association of Writers union. He and his second wife, Vera, moved into a two-room apartment with Elena and her son. Alexei remained committed to Marxism, but he grew more at odds with the Soviet government. He became a vocal humanitarian advocate for nationalities such as the Crimean Tatars that he felt were wrongly treated in their homelands or forced into exile by the Soviets. He tried to spread the word about their situation and lobby for better treatment.

Alexei "helped me comprehend the needs of the country and the many ways in which the people were suffering," wrote his close friend, ex-Major General Petro Grigorenko. "Having spent the Civil War and the first post-war years in the northern Caucasus, he had been bound by a multitude of ties to the small groups living there."

A new USSR leader, Leonid Brezhnev, replaced Khrushchev in 1964. Alexei continued to speak out against certain Soviet policies and complained about the "re-Stalinization" of Russia. His views earned him the attention of the

KGB, the new Soviet intelligence agency. The KGB investigated his activities. The Party ejected him once again, but then reinstated him because of a reluctance to prosecute old Communists and former Stalin prisoners.

The year 1968 was significant for Nina's family. Alexei hosted a controversial meeting of human rights activists early in the year and protested the Soviet invasion of Czechoslovakia in the spring. "He left the Party and tore the Party membership card," Elena said. "It was a very difficult decision for him. He was a participant of the revolution and underground work. So the card meant much for him."

In March, the Crimean Tatar population held a celebration to honor Alexei's 72nd birthday. Suffering from a deteriorating heart condition, he was too ill to attend but sent Grigorenko, who accepted the honor on Alexei's behalf with a fiery speech about human rights violations. Grigorenko was another well-known dissident out of favor with the government. He later fled to the United States and published his memoir outlining political troubles in this era of the Soviet Union.

In June 1968, an American publisher, Crown Books, released Nina's diary translated into English.

That October, Alexei was once again expelled from the Party and Association of Writers. He wrote a final, politically outspoken article from his hospital bed and apparently avoided arrest only because of his serious illness. He died November 10. His funeral was symbolic of his hard-core revolutionary life, causing quite a stir when it became a showdown between the hundreds of mourners and the KGB worried about the event becoming a political rally. "After decades of suffocating silence, the first free public meeting had taken place," Grigorenko wrote in describing what the mourners felt they achieved during Alexei's memorial service. "My friend could be proud. Even in death, he had inspired the democratic movement in our country."

The KGB held Alexei's letters and other writings in its archives for the next twenty-five years.

Nina's Impact in America

Nina's diary, meanwhile, received much interest with its English version. American teens liked Nina's story.

Young people participating in New York literary cafes said they liked the lack of sentimentality in Nina's writing, something they felt worsened some Soviet books. They also appreciated it not being written in an archaic language that made it difficult to enjoy the storyline. Some felt moved by Nina's descriptions of Moscow. And many valued Nina's belief that the future would not forgive young people for sitting on the sidelines as passive observers in important events. They quoted her comparison to the trees she so admired in the forests around Moscow: "And I feel, like these proud pine trees are telling me: 'You have to live your life so that you will have a right to hold your head like us—high, proudly, independently.'"

The U.S. Union of Libraries recommended *The Diary of Nina Kosterina* as one of the best 50 books for young people in 1968. Book reviewers liked it as well.

"The flamingly honest self-portrait will invite comparison with another ill-fated diarist (Anne Frank), but it deserves to stand alone, imparting one girl's hungering for love, culture, action, involvement," a reviewer from The *Horn Book* magazine covering children's literature wrote in an excerpt included on the book cover.

A *New York Times* newspaper reviewer wrote in December 1968 that the diary's appeal came from being about the personal feelings of an average person rather than about politics, slogans and propaganda. It didn't represent a propaganda poster, the *Times* reviewer wrote, but a real Soviet life.

Russians who immigrated to the United States hoped Nina's story would explain to Americans the realities of what they called ezhovshina. Even their U.S.-

born children couldn't always grasp the horrors described by their parents and thought their 1930s stories were exaggerated a bit. Ezhov was the last name of a minister of internal affairs during Stalin's time whose "second job" was to arrest enemies of the state, usually at night with no explanation. Picking up on a Russian practice to call time periods by the last names of important figures, this era of illegal arrests became known as ezhovshina since Minister Ezhov apparently took an important role in these night arrests.

Nina's Gift to New Generations

Both parents were gone by the time the demand for Nina's diary prompted a second printing in English in 1977. Nina's mother, Anna, died of cancer in 1974. "Mama stayed in the hospital for a long time," Elena recalled. "However, it became clear that there was no hope of recovery. So we took her home. She died asleep."

Nina's sisters, cousin Stella and friend Lena watched as interest in Nina continued. Playwrights even turned Nina's diary into two separate productions performed in Moscow theaters in the mid-1980s.

"I found a theater playbill of the first night performance…October 14, 1984…The performance was called 'You Will Always Be. A Diary of Nina Kosterina,'" Elena remembered. Elena, Vera and Stella visited a second production staged in two other Moscow theaters, too. The producer "was very much surprised when he found out that Nina's sisters were still alive . . . People from the theater got acquainted with us, took photos," Elena said. She later learned that the play was performed in the Urals as well.

Their cousin Irma had died by this time. Nina's youngest sister, Vera, passed away in 1997 and Elena eventually lost touch with Lena. But Elena continued to call Moscow home, as did their cousin Stella. Elena and her son became the keepers of the family's archive of photos, Nina's original diary and other bits of memories. Elena and Stella, unable to move about the city much, stayed in contact by phone.

Nina's story continues to emerge in research papers about the Stalin era and books about young people's diaries. And the Kosterin activist spirit continues in Elena's son, Alexey—Nina's nephew and Alexei's grandson. He reported spending twelve years as a political prisoner through the 1980s and early 1990s. An engineer by training, he has become an outspoken advocate for humanitarian causes. In 1993, the KGB returned Alexei Kosterin's materials to his grandson's care and Alexey arranged for their permanent storage at the Central Memorial Society in Moscow. He readily helped his mother in sharing the family's history and he displayed pride in the young, idealistic, gutsy aunt he never knew.

Nina was indeed an ordinary girl in many ways, yet she responded to extraordinary times with a sense of ethics, an unquenchable quest for knowledge and the ability to show courage when faced with fear. Her story provides inspiration and instruction for new generations of ordinary girls and boys who might face their own extraordinary situations, big or small, in the years to come.

Glossary

Bolshevik—Means "One of the Majority." This name was used by Vladimir Lenin and the faction of the Russian Social-Democratic Workers' Party that seized control of government in 1917. The Bolsheviks later changed their name to the Russian Communist Party (of Bolsheviks), then to the All-Union Communist Party (of Bolsheviks), and eventually to the Communist Party of the Soviet Union.

Bourgeoisie—To be labeled politically unreliable and holding on to non-Communist beliefs. People not falling into "worker" classes most often earned this label, such as priests, people with past wealth and upper-class ties, property and factory owners, and those in white-collar or intellectual jobs.

Censorship—Restrictions on the information that citizens can access.

Communism—A political and economic system in which property is owned by the state or community and all citizens are supposed to share in the common wealth, more or less according to their need.

Five-Year Plans—A method begun by Joseph Stalin and used in the late 1920s and early 1930s to communicate the Soviet government's vision and major strategies to achieve the vision.

Gulag—The type of Russian labor camp used to imprison criminals and political enemies. Gulag is an acronym for the Russian words, Chief Administration of Corrective Labor Camps.

Komsomol—The Young Communist League, which had members from ages fourteen to twenty-eight who trained to spread Communist teachings and prepare for future membership in the Communist Party. The Communists organized the Komsomol in 1918 to bring together different youth organizations involved in the Russian Revolution. When Communism collapsed in the Soviet Union, so did the Komsomol. It disbanded in 1991.

Little Octoberists—The Communist Party youth branch for ages eight to eleven.

Marxism—A system and philosophy of economics based on the idea of the collective good and a society without different levels of privilege, developed by Karl Marx and Friedrich Engels in the mid-19th century. Various movements have used Marxism as a foundation for their beliefs, leading to Socialism, Leninism, Communism and other variations.

October Revolution—This actually involved two revolutions to overthrow the Russian monarchy. The first happened in February 1917 by the traditional Russian calendar (March 1917 by the new calendar used by most countries) when the imperial government was removed. The second happened October 24-25 (November 6-7 according to the traditional Russian calendar) when the Bolsheviks occupied all strategic buildings, transportation and communication points to assume control over the country.

Partisan—Someone who aligns themselves closely with a military action or political cause.

Partizanka—The word used to describe young Soviet women who became partisan heroines fighting behind enemy lines during World War II.

Socialist—Another term to describe a person, group or action believing in collective ownership and basic principles developed by Karl Marx, perhaps with variations on what Marx originally proposed.

USSR—The organization of separate Russia and Baltic states in 1922 into one country called the Union of Soviet Socialist Republics, or Soviet Union. Its territory was the largest in the world, stretching from the Baltic and Black seas to the Pacific Ocean and, in its final years, consisting of 15 Soviet Socialist Republics.

By December 1991, the USSR had virtually ceased to exist as the government structure came apart and several states began declaring their independence.

Young Pioneers—Another Communist Party youth branch, also known as the All-Union Lenin Pioneer Organization, for ages nine to fourteen. It was established in 1922.

Notes on Key Sources

There are many books and library database articles explaining the Russian revolution, Vladimir Lenin and Joseph Stalin. A few that I found especially helpful included:

★ Colton, Timothy J. Moscow. *Governing the Socialist Metropolis.* Cambridge, Massachusetts: The Belknap Press of Harvard University Press, 1995.

★ Fitzpatrick, Sheila. *Everyday Stalinism: Ordinary Life in Extraordinary Times: Soviet Russia in the 1930s.* Oxford Press, 2000.

★ Furst, Juliane. "Heroes, Lovers, Victims—Partisan Girls during the Great Fatherland War." Minerva: Quarterly

Report on Women and the Military. Fall-Winter, 2000.

★ Gottfried, Ted. *The Stalinist Empire*. Brookfield, Connecticut: The Millbrook Press, Inc., 2002.

★ Kirschenbaum, Lisa. *Small Comrades: Revolutionizing Childhood in Soviet Russia, 1917-1932*. Garland Publishing, Inc., 2000.

To find out more about Nina's life, I enlisted the help of the Blitz research agency in Russia to search for family and archived documents. I was excited to learn that one of Nina's sisters was still living in Moscow, along with Nina's nephew and his family. This led to interviews with Elena Alexeevna Kosterina (Nina's sister) and Alexey Smirnov (Nina's nephew), in Moscow during November-December 2004, conducted by a Russian researcher and transcribed into English. The family also shared the photographs included in this book and information contained in documents they had saved over the years. I am extremely grateful to Elena and Alexey for being so helpful and willing to share information about Nina and their family.

I also found valuable information about Nina and the family in the following sources:

★ Biography-Bibliography Dictionary: "Writers of the Current Epoch," Pisateli sovremennoi epokhi. Biobibliograficheski slovar, Volume 3, Moscow, 1995. Prepared for publication by N.A. Bogomolov

★ Ginsburg, Mirra. Personal Papers, Children's Literature Research Collection, University of Minnesota, which includes notes about the book and a photocopy of a Radio Liberty-Moscow transcript in Russian about the release of diary in United States

★ Kassil', Lev, "Her Big, Invincible World," foreword published in *The Diary of Nina Kosterina*, Russian version, 1964

★ Kosterin, Alexei Evgrafovich. Afterword published in *The Diary of Nina Kosterina*, Russian version, 1964

★ Russian National Library Manuscript Department Fond 103 file 79 (archive of G.G. Brodersen), biographical questionnaire on A.E. Kosterin for the Dictionary of Contemporaries publication

And, last but not least, I drew heavily from the English version of Nina's diary, translated by Mirra Ginsburg and released by Crown Publishers in New York in 1968. I obtained permission from

Ms. Ginsburg's estate to use copyrighted excerpts from her English translation of various diary entries. The original diary in its four copybooks remains with Elena Kosterina. Mirra Ginsburg's personal papers at Columbia University in New York include a Russian transcript of the diary.

Image sources were as follows:

★ All images of Nina, her family and friends were provided by Nina's family

★ Art book covers on p. 110 and Soviet war poster on p. 152 are courtesy of the author

★ The Maxim Gorky stamp image on p. 111 and Mayakovsky statue image on p. 113 are stock images purchased from 123RF.com

About the Author

Jennifer Phillips writes stories that celebrate creativity, courage and determination. She loves opportunities to connect with readers of all ages about her books, as well as people on their own writing journeys.

Visit her website at www.jenniferphillipsauthor.com for free extras about Nina Kosterina and the subjects of her other books. Sign up for her newsletter to get book- related updates and explore how creative problem-solving techniques can help in your writing and in life.